CONCEPTS OF MESSIAH

A study of the Messianic Concepts of
Islam,
Judaism,
Messianic Judaism
and Christianity

Yehoiakin ben Ya'ocov

WestBow
PRESS
A DIVISION OF THOMAS NELSON

Copyright © 2012 by Yehoiakin ben Ya'ocov.

All rights reserved. No part of this book may be used or reproduced by any means, graphic, electronic, or mechanical, including photocopying, recording, taping or by any information storage retrieval system without the written permission of the publisher except in the case of brief quotations embodied in critical articles and reviews.

ISBN: 978-1-4497-5744-1 (sc)
ISBN: 978-1-4497-5745-8 (e)
ISBN: 978-1-4497-5746-5 (hc)

Library of Congress Control Number: 2012912227

WestBow Press books may be ordered through booksellers or by contacting:

WestBow Press
A Division of Thomas Nelson
1663 Liberty Drive
Bloomington, IN 47403
www.westbowpress.com
1-(866) 928-1240

Unless otherwise noted, all Scripture quotations are taken from the Complete Jewish Bible, copyright © 1998 by David H. Stern. Published by Jewish New Testament Publications, Inc. www.messianicjewish.net/jntp. Distributed by Messianic Jewish Resources. www.messianicjewish.net. All rights reserved. Used by permission.

Scripture quotations marked (LEB) are from the Lexham English Bible. Copyright 2012 Logos Bible Software. Lexham is a registered trademark of Logos Bible Software.

Because of the dynamic nature of the Internet, any web addresses or links contained in this book may have changed since publication and may no longer be valid. The views expressed in this work are solely those of the author and do not necessarily reflect the views of the publisher, and the publisher hereby disclaims any responsibility for them.

Any people depicted in stock imagery provided by Thinkstock are models, and such images are being used for illustrative purposes only.

Certain stock imagery © Thinkstock.

Printed in the United States of America

WestBow Press rev. date: 07/12/12

Dedication

I wish to dedicate this book to my good friend and brother in the Messiah of Israel Tracy J. Lebret, from Wellpinte, Washington. May you name be forever counted as one of the righteous men of our times. May you and your family be blessed by the G-d of Avraham, Yitzaak Ya-ocov.

Shalom.

Contents

Introduction ix
Definitions xi
Behold The Mahdi. 1
Mochiach Ben Dovid 24
Mochiach Ben Elohim 42
Jesus The Christ, ... 100
Mochiach Ha Chaim Torah 127
Conclusion 133
Appendix I 135
Appendix II 142
Appendix III 147
Bibliography 160
Jewish Source Material 162
Christian source material 164
Historical and other Source Material 166

Introduction

What is a messiah? We hear this word a lot these days. We see it in the pages of history. It echoes down through the ages. The word, the idea, and the concept is thrown around by churchmen, clerics, priests. rabbis, ayatollahs, mullahs, and the laymen of the three monotheistic religions. The monotheistic religions, are *Judaism, Christianity,* and *Islam*. And then there is the revived, Messianic Judaism, which many traditional Jews consider to be a form of Christianity while the Christians consider it to be a part of Judaism. I am a Messianic Jew, and I am of the firm conviction that Messianic Judaism is part of Judaism. Furthermore it is a return to biblical Judaism.

The third monotheistic religion, *Islam* comes in many sects, but its two main divisions are *Sunni* and *Shi'ite*. Their word for messiah is, **Mahdi**. It is not my intention to discuss all of the differences and doctrines of Islam in great detail, nor is it my intention in this writing to discus cover the differences between the many denominations of Christianity or those of traditional Judaism. Rather this first section focuses on what each of these groups considers a messiah to be, and what their expectations are, regarding his coming, as in the case of traditional Judaism and Islam, or his return, as in the case of **Messianic Judaism** and Christianity.

This book deals with, in brief, a specialized Concept of the Messiah, called ***Living Torah***. Living Torah is an especially Messianic Jewish concept dealt with this extensively in another book titled, *"Torah Is Calling."* But it is necessary to cover some of this ground again, because it is an important concept of messiah. In my belief, it is the **most important** of all the *Concepts of Messiah*.

When I started this writing it was the second day of Passover on the fifteenth day of the Month of Nisan, year 5770 on the Jewish calendar.

This corresponded to March 31st, 2010. For Messianic Jews, this season of Passover, not only represents our liberation from bondage in Egypt by the hand of Almighty G-d, but our liberation from bondage to sin by the Messiah. This is a Messianic Season. A Season of Messiah. I will be dealing with the concept of the Season of Messiah in detail in the last half in the Living Torah portion of this booklet. It is a vital concept that all of us need to know and to remember, and take to heart.

I find it tragic that people in Christianity have been taught to ignore all of the Biblical Feasts ,replacing them with Pagan aberrations, which have been given new names. They claim to worship the Messiah of the Passover, but brush it all aside, taking not even one moment to remember, that their Messiah is part and parcel of Judaism, and that he was a Master Rabbi.

They overlook this fact,offering weak explanations, while working on all these biblical Sabbaths or having a party on vacations.

It is time for a change. Welcome to the study, and may G-d richly bless all those who read this and apply it

Shalom.

Definitions

First of all, we need to define what the word messiah means. Only then can we take the next step up the ladder. Without a correct definition, we cannot take the next step up on the ladder as to who the Messiah is, and what his purpose is. In each of the concepts of messiah, he has a different purpose. Islam, Judaism, Christianity, all have different concepts and this of course let us know that in each one, the purpose of, and role of the Messiah is different, as is his nature. His person and his nature of purpose is different, but the endgame is the same. A Messianic Global Empire.

The word itself means, *"Anointed One"*. It comes from the Hebrew word, *"Mochiach.* The Aramaic form is, *"Meshiha."* The Arabic word is *"Masih"* and the Greek form is *"Messias."* So from where do the Christians get this word, *"Christ"*? The word Christ is the English adaptation of the word, *"Christos,"* which is also Greek. It is a word that is used 40 times in the Septuagint, which was the first non-Hebrew translation of the Jewish Tanakh. It was translated around the year 247 B.C.E. The Septuagint (from the Latin septuaginta, meaning, "seventy" and frequently referred to by the Roman Numerals LXX) The name derives from the tradition that it was made by seventy (or seventy-two) Jewish Scribes at Alexandria, Egypt during the reign of Pharaoh Ptolemy Philadephus. It has been preserved in a large number of manuscript copies of the original.

The Arabic word ,*"Mahdi"* (pronounced, maha-dee) which is a title meaning*"The Guided One"*and carries with it a slightly different concept than the word messiah carries.

As we now go into the meanings and definition of these different concepts of messiah, you are going to discover many similarities and some stark differences. Also some mirror images. Seemingly the same at first glance, but completely opposite in outcome, and character. Some stand for peace, justice honor and salvation, while others stand for violence and bloodshed, and are the harbinger of the Apocalypse! Where is the messiah in your own, spiritual life? Are you filled with the Holy Spirit of G-d, or on the verge of your own personal *Armageddon?* The choice stands before you now. Will it be life, or will it be death? Will it be an afterlife of *Gan-Eden* (Heavenly Paradise) or *Sheol* and *Gehinnom*. (The grave and judgment) I ask this to illustrate how important it is for you personally to know, the concepts of messiah and the Living Torah.

Behold The Mahdi.

In view of the ongoing war with the Islamic Underground,which may at some point involve Islamic Persia (Iran) led by the Supreme Leader, Grand Ayatollah Ali Kahmani and President of the Islamic Republic, Ahmadinejad, it is important to understand the Islamic concept of messiah:. First let me show you something curious. If you consider the root word of the name of the Iranian president, and you will discover the word, *mahdi*. (Ah-**madi**-dinejad) I am not declaring that this man is the Shi'ite Messiah,but I am merely bringing this thought to mind, in light of the fact that this man wishes to destroy Israel with atomic weapons. Many of Islam's followers wish to bring about conditions worldwide, that they believe will usher in the age of the Islamic Messiah

The following definitions are very important if one is to begin to understand Islam.

- DAJJAL. The last of a line of 30 false prophets who will arise. This one will be defeated by the Mahdi.

- DAR AL HARB. The House of War. This is the Islamic term for all those areas of the world which are not under the control of Islamic Governments.

- DAR AL ISLAM. The House of Submission. The area of the world which is under the submission of Islamic Governments and Religion. Sometime also referred to the,"House of Peace."

- GHAZI Turkish Islamic Jihadist fighter. Units of these were used by the Ottoman Empire to expand Islam. These units were fierce fighters who were willing to become Shihadahs for Allah and Islam.

- HIDDEN IMAM: Abu Al-Qasim Mohammed. The 12th Imam of the Shi'ah. Went into hiding in 874 C.E. In 934 his *"Occultation"* was declared. Allah it was said, had concealed the Imam, and that shortly before the last judgment, he would return as the Mahdi. Upon his return, he will usher in a golden age a

- IMAM. An Islam religious and prayer leader in the Sunni community. In Shi'ite Islam this is a term used to denote descendents of Mohammed the Prophet his daughter **Fatima** and her husband and Nephew of **Mohammed, Ali ibn Ali Talib**. The sects of Shi'ite Islam consider these and their decedents to be the true successors of the Prophet.

- JIHAD Islamic Holy War commanded by the Qur'an, "Fight and slay the pagans." While some have tried to interpret Jihad as an internal personal struggle against the evil I ones own life, the Hadith is very clear that Jihad is a religious war against those nations who will not submit to Muslim rule and convert to Islam. Ahmadiyya Islam teaches that Jihad refers to a struggle against the devil and ones low desires and to the peaceful prop of Islam with special emphasis being placed on the spreading of the Islamic faith by being living examples.

- JIZYA. A poll tax paid by non-Muslim religious groups living in Islamic Nations. This is a means by which Islam allows Christian and Jewish communities to exist without conversion to Islam and without their death. It is a discriminatory religious tax whereby the Muslim rulers extort money from the infidel instead of beheading them. peace, after having destroyed the enemies of Allah, in the final Jihad

- MIDRASA An Islamic Religious School where students memorize the Qur'an and are taught the Hadith and

Shariah law. Discipline is ofter very harsh and includes shackling and beatings for mistakes. Only men and boys are allowed. No women or girls.

- MUJAHAD. An Islamic Holy Warrior fighting against the enemies of Islam and to conquer non-Muslim nations and peoples.

- MUJAHADEEN. Military units of Islamic Jihadist fighters

- MUJADDID. A divine reformer foretold in Islamic Prophecy.

- QA'EM (He who Arises) A Shi'ite Messianic figure, sometimes refereed to as the Mahdi.

- SHARIAH (Path to the Watering hole) This is the body of Islamic law and jurisprudence, which has its origins in the Hadith and is the system which governs not only the Islamic State, but every aspect of the lives of every single person subject to Islam. It is the goal of the Islamic Jihadists to conquer the world and bring every person and nation in the world under Shariah law.

- SHIHADAH A Muslim martyr. A suicide bomber or other person who kills Jews or Christians and others who will not convert to Islam, and loose their own life in the process

- SOFYANI. A Muslim tyrant that will oppose and do battle with the Mahdi in Syria and Iraq.

The Hadith speaks of him as a wicked ruler who will spread crime and corruption around the earth just before the advent of the Mahdi.

- SUNNAH: It means, custom, and refers to the habits and the religious practices of the Prophet Mohammed. These are enshrined into Islamic Law, as related in the Hadith.

- ULAMA: Learned men.
- UMMAH: The Muslim Community.
- ZIMMI A non-Muslim or an Infidel.

The Islamic concepts of messiah, are broken into three dominant sects,

1. Sunni
2. Shi'ite
3. Ahmadiyya

We will deal with each one of these in the order listed above and I hope by the end of this that the reader will have a good basic understanding of these concepts of messiah.

While I am not here judge every follower of the Islamic Faith, I will declare this. Islam claims to venerate our Torah, and by extension the entire Bible. In the Torah, it is forbidden to commit murder and assault. Yet this is allowed in the **Qur'an**, which is the scriptures of Islam, and in the **Hadith,** which is the written oral tradition of Islam. This gains full embodiment in their concept of, *"Jihad"* or, *"Holy War."* The Hadith is the written Oral Traditions of Islam, without it to guide them, Muslims cannot properly interpret their scriptures. These are listed in the bibliography at the end of the book The major one in use is the, **Sahih Muslim,** codified during the late middle ages by the Imam Muslim. It is widely used in the system of Islamic Religious education. These schools are know as, Midrasas, and are cold, harsh and austere. Especially in the Sudan, boys are forced to memorize the Qur'an and are beaten with whips and canes for mistakes.

We shall now learn the Sunni Muslim concept of Messiah. Sunni Islam is the predominate branch of Islam which is prevalent across the Arabian peninsula, Eastern Palestine (Jordan) and Syria, North Africa and in Afghanistan and Pakistan.

From Wikipedia.

The Sunnis view the Mahdi as the successor of Prophet Mohammad, the Mahdi is expected to arrive to rule the world and he is to reestablish uprightness, harmony, and correct religion. The definite term mahdi, means "the rightly-guided one". The Mahdi is not mentioned in the Qur'ān, but rather in the Sunnah. Some hypothesise he came about when the Arabian tribes were settling in Syria under Mo'awiya. "They anticipated 'the Mahdi who will lead the rising people of the Yemen back to their country' in order to restore the glory of their lost Himyarite kingdom. It was believed that he would eventually conquer Constantinople."

Two other notions that became thoroughly related with the belief in the Mahdi. The first was the notion of return of the dead, particularly of the Imams. The second was the indication of occultation. "When Mohammad bin. al-Ḥanafiya died in 700, the Kaysāniya maintained that he was in occultation in the Raẓwā mountains west of Medina, and would one day return as the Mahdi." The appearance of the Prophet was also proposed unto the Mahdi. "An enormously influential tradition attributed to 'Abd-Allāh b. Mas'ud has MoḤammad predict the coming of a Mahdi coined in his own image: 'His name will be my name, and his father's name my father's name'"

For many *Sunnis*, after the reign of the Mahdi, Isa will return to battle a false messiah sent by Satan. *Isa* is the Arabic name for Yeshua Ha Notzri, who is known to much of the world as Jesus of Nazareth. They believe that Yeshua (Jesus) was born of a virgin, Miriam. However, he was not, in their view, the Son of G-d. For it is stated in the Qur'an, G-d does not procreate. He does not begot, nor was he begotten. They believe that he was spoken into being, inside the womb of Miriam (Mary) and is considered, along with Moses, to be a *Prophet* of G-d. They believe, that on the day of judgment, Isa will return from heaven as a Muslim. He will triumph over the Anti-Christ at Armageddon, then destroy all the *Cross Worshipers*. This is of course, a code word for the Christians. He will break up all of their crosses like he would any other idols. Ram Swarup in his book on the Hadith points out that the Prophet Muhammad's idea of Isa, (Yeshua – Jesus) was that he would return as a *mujhid* (crusader or holy warrior) waging war against the Christians and the Jews as well as other non-Muslims. It is declared by the Hadith in the book, *Iman (Faith)*;

> "The son of Mary will soon descend among you as a just judge. He will break crosses, kill swine, and abolish *jizya*"

Dr. Ram Swarup also explained the above verse on page 24 of his book saying

> Mohamed proclaims. How? The translator explains, "Cross is a symbol of Christianity. Jesus will break this symbol after the advent of Mohammed. Islam is the *din* (religion) of Allah and no other religion is acceptable to him. Similarly, the flesh of swine is a favorite dish of the Christians. Jesus will sweep out of existence this dirty and loathsome animal. The whole of the human race would accept Islam and there will be no *zimmis* left and this *jizya* would be automatically abolished" Jesus is regarded as just judge, but this only means that he will judge according to the shariah of Mohammed. For, as the translator explains, 'the Shariah of all the earlier prophets stands abrogated with the advent of Muhammad's Apostleship. Jesus will, therefore, judge according to the law of Islam.

I find it interesting that during his 7 year reign, the Mahdi is unable to bring the enemies of Islam to submission, and so Allah has to send Isa, This is reminiscent of the Beast and the False Prophet in the Bible.

The term *jizya* refers to a discriminatory poll tax that non-Muslims are forced to pay according to Islamic law, and a *zimmi* is a non-Muslim or and infidel

Book 39 of the Hadith speaks of the end of days and the turmoils and upheaval during the days of the Mahdi and has something foreboding concerning the Jewish people

Concepts of Messiah

"The last hour would not come unless the Muslims will fight against the Jews and the Muslims would kill them and until the Jews would hide themselves behind a stone or a tree and a stone or a tree would say: Muslim, or the servant of Allah, there is a Jew behind me; come and kill him"

It also speaks of a thorny tree called the *gharqad* as the only tree which would remain loyal to the Jewish people and not reveal there location to the Islamic Jihadists,

In modern times, many Muslims are claiming that Yeshua was not Jewish, but was a Palestinian Arab. This in spite of all historical evidence to the contrary, such as the works of the Jewish Historian, Flavius Josephus. I believe this concept of messiah is to be racist and bigoted. These are the same group of fanatics who deny that the Jews have a right to live in Judea and the rest of Israel, simply because we are not Muslims and are Jews!

I am sure that there are other Sunni views of the Mahdi, but now I want to move on into the Shi'ite concept of messiah. What sets the Shi'ites apart from the Sunnis? The Sunnis, which includes the sect called, *Wahabis*, of which the late Osama Bin Laden, Iman Al Zawahiri, and much of the Al Qaeda Jihadist network belong, can be considered to be the Orthodox branch of Islam. Wahhabis being the Ultra-orthodox. There are also the Sufis, which are the Islamic Mystics. From the Sufis come the Dervishes, who dance whirling dances in order to be drawn into the Mystical realms of Allah.

Shi'ite Islam separated quite early in Islamic History from the mainstream. They are by no means small fringe group. There are millions of them, constituting the majority of Muslims in both Iraq and Iran.

After the death of the Prophet Mohammed, the leadership of the Muslim community passed into the hands of what are known as the, *Rashidun*,.(Rightly Guided Caliphs). The word, *Caliph*, means, *Companion*, and refers to the four main companions of Mohammed, one of whom was , OMAR. It was he who led the first Jihad. This happened in the late 5th Century C.E. It was a war in which all of Persia was conquered, along with the land of Israel and Syria, Egypt, and later in the early 6th century, all of North Africa and Spain. Even the Frankish Kingdom (France) was invaded. They were stopped by Charles Martel, King of the Franks, at the Battle of Tours, and forced back across the Pyrenees Mountains into Spain. The lands of the Eastern and Southern Mediterranean Sea passed from the rule of the Orthodox Christian, Eastern Roman(Byzantine) Empire, and remain Muslim to this day. That is except Jerusalem and the land of Israel, which has been liberated from the Islamic boot

Upon the death of Mohammed, a group arose called, **Shiah al Ali.** (Partisans of Ali). They believed that *Ali ibn Ali Talib* the nephew and Son-in-law of Mohammed, was lawful heir. He was Mohammed's closest male relative. The *Shiah-i-ali* believed that Ali's leadership of the Muslim Community was usurped by Omar and the companions and a split occurred, which remains to this day. There is much hatred between these groups, as we can see by that fact that Al Qaeda has been bombing Shi'ite Mosques in Iraq, ever since the USA liberated that land from the Murderous Rule of Saddam Hussein. Hussein was a Sunni and has hung for his vicious crimes against humanity.

The nation of Iran, which until 1935 was called Persia, is ruled by a Twelver Shi'ite regime and the law of the land is Shariah. The official name of the country is, **"The Islamic Republic of Iran."** Not all of the Persians are supporters of this Jihadist regime. The massive protest demonstrations across Iran in 2009-2010 prove this. Ahmahdinejad and the Twelver Shi'ites believe, as part of their end-time eschatology, that the return of the Mahdi is soon. However, they must usher in the global chaos which will make his arrival possible. A Great Mosque has been constructed in Teheran, Iran from which they believe he will rule the world. He will appear in Mecca first, and then march north to battle the enemies of Allah. He will destroy the cross worshipers,and as the rocks cry out, "Oh Muslim, there is a Jew hiding behind me! Come and kill him!"

The Mahdi will destroy all the Jews, whom Allah has cursed because they rejected Mohammed as a Prophet, and would not convert to Islam. At this time, the Shitan, Satan, shall send the false Mahdi down from the sky. It will be then, that the Mahdi will gather all the armies of Islam, from the four corners of the earth. They shall do battle against the False Mahdi and destroy him. Once this is accomplished, all the Muslims, the Sunnis, who have rejected the Mahdi, will themselves be destroyed and cast into hell. Now, according to this doctrine, there have been six great prophets since the dawn of time. These men were:

1. Adam
2. Noah
3. Abraham
4. Moses
5. Isa (Jesus)
6. Mohammed

Each one of these Prophets had a companion, or executor, who taught the deep, secret, and esoteric meanings of what had been revealed to the Prophet by Allah, to those men who were capable, and deemed worthy of receiving it. The periods of time between each of these Prophets, had been a down-ward spiral of mankind's spiritual elevation. So Allah would send each Prophet, in an attempt to reverse this trend. Aaron had been the executor of Moses and Ali had been that of Mohammed. And so as the followers of the true faith attempted and struggled to put these teachings into practice, they would be preparing the world for the final judgment, which would then usher in the reign of justice, which will be inaugurated by the seventh prophet: the Mahdi

I found the following material at Wikipedia, the online free encyclopedia. The article is quite detailed and I recommend it for those who want more details on the Mahdi and the doctrines surrounding him.

The end of time and rising of the Mahdi- The "end of time" or the date of the ultimate arrival of the Hidden Imam, is unknown and followers are insisted to anticipate liberation tolerantly and virtuously. The future approaching of the Savior is the most recurrently quoted topic in prophecies made by the Prophet, Faṭima, and the Imams: complete extensive chapters are devoted to the subject in the sources. This future is foreshadowed by a number of signs. The widespread signs are the prevalent invasion of the earth by Wicked, the overpowering of knowledge by unawareness, and the loss of a intelligence of the blessed and all that associates man to God and his neighbors. These, in some degree, require the demonstration and the rising of the Qāʾem, or else mortality will be astounded by obscurity. "Furthermore, there are certain specific signs among which five recur more regularly and are hence justifiably called the "five signs":

- The coming of Sofyāni, the enemy of the Qāʾem, who will command an army in battle against the latter

- The advent of Yamāni, who appears in the Yemen to preach support for the Qāʾem;

- The Cry/Scream of supernatural origin, coming from the sky and calling man to defend the Imam's cause;

- The swallowing of an army composed of the Imam's enemies in a desert often located between Mecca and Medina, according to a hadith most likely propagated by ʿAbd-Allāh b. Zobayr during his war propaganda against the Umayyad caliph Yazid , during the latter's campaign against Mecca and Medina, popularized by the traditionist of Basra, Qatāda and

- The assassination by the Meccans of the messenger to the Qā'em, often called Nafs or al-Nafs al-Zakiya (echoing the messianic rebellion and death in 762 of the Hasanid Moḥammad b. 'Abd-Allāh, surnamed al-Nafs al-Zakiya)."

The Mahdi accordingly becomes visible, all the while having inexplicably kept his youth. He combats and ultimately deracinates Evil, re-establishing the world to its novel wholesome state. For this to happen, he must first retaliate the slaying of Imam Ḥosayn in order that the common of Muslims be removed of the wicked corruption that it ever committed. Furthermore, according to the eschatological guideline of raj'a, a definite number of previous saints, fatalities of their society's prejudice, and their oppressors originate back to life in order that the moral may take retaliation on the malicious ones. The Redeemer will so not only re-establish Islam, but all faiths, to their wholesomeness and new veracity, creating "submission to God" the worldwide religion. The Mahdi will also open up the deep esoteric secrets of Islamic Scriptures. The whole world will be taken to submission. Powers of inequality and obliviousness will be all eliminated, the earth will be inflated with justice and wisdom, and mortality revitalized by knowledge. The Mahdi accordingly formulates the world for the last trial of the ultimate reappearance of the Last Judgment. According to some traditions, the Mahdi will be in control upon the earth for certain time , seven, nine or nineteen 7, 9, 19 years, after which ensues the death of all civilization just preceding the Judgment. Other traditions state subsequently the demise of the Qā'em, the régime of the world will continue in the influences of the initiated for a definite period before the Day of Resurrection.

There is another branch of Shi'ite Islam, known as, Sevener Shi'ites. They believe in the same way regarding the end times as do the Twelvers. But with some key differences. The Seveners are also known as the "ISMAILIS." who believe that the line of Ali ended with the

7th Imam, the Imam Ismail. This because they do not recognize the legitimacy of his son, Musa Al Kazim, who is revered as the 7th Imam by the Twelvers. But it is clear, that both groups believe the Mahdi to be a decedent of Imam Ali Ibn Abu Talib, who was both the son-in-law, and the nephew of Mohammed, the Prophet of Islam.

Mahdi is a normal man who is going to follow the true Islam. He is not the son of Allah. Islam is an absolute monotheistic religion and they consider to be blasphemy, any doctrine which teaches that Allah has a son. . His name will be Muhammad and his father name will be 'Abdullah. He is a descendant from Ali and Fatima (daughter of the prophet Muhammad) so he will be descendant from al-Hasan or al-Husain. Mahdi will be very just and his capital will be Damascus. Shi'ite Islam teaches that Allah declared that Jews will master the world two times and the Mahdi will appear between those two periods and will rule through the last one. The Mahdi is not considered to be a prophet but he is the final Rightly Guided Caliph.. Mahdi will lead Muslims to a great victory against the Christian Romans (i.e. All the white Europeans including the Americans). This great war is called al-Malhamah al-Kubrah or Armageddon. It will end up with a great victory to Muslims against Romans after six years. Muslims will take over their capital Rome (this can be any city). In the seventh year, the Anticrist will apear and a greater war will start between Jews and Muslims for 40 days (longer that usual days) and will end when Jesus will come and Muslims will kill all Jews. All people will convert into Islam. Peace will pervade the whole world.

The following material is drawn from Wikipedia.
Mohammed said:
The Mahdi is the protector of the knowledge, the heir to the knowledge of all the prophets and is aware of all things. The dominion (authority) of the Mahdi is one of the proofs that God has created all things;these are so numerous that his [the Mahdi's] proofs will overcome (will be influential, will be dominant) everyone and nobody will have any counter-proposition against him. People will flee from him [the

Mahdi] as sheep flee from the shepherd. Later, people will begin to look for a purifier. But since they can find none to help them but him, they will begin to run to him When matters are entrusted to competent [the Mahdi], Almighty God will raise the lowest .part of the world for him, and lower the highest places. So much that he will see the whole world as if in the palm of his hand. Which of you cannot see even a single hair in the palm of his hand? In the time of the Mahdi, a Muslim in the East will be able to see his Muslim brother in the West, and he in the West will see him in the East

Sadir al-Sayrafi says: I heard from Imam Abu Abdullah Jafar al-Sadiq that: ... He whose rights have been taken away and who is denied (hazrat* mahdi (as)) will walk among them, move through their markets and walk where they walk. but they will not recognize hazrat mahdi (as) until Allah gives them leave to recognize him, just as He did with the Prophet Yusuf (as).

- *Hazrat means "(His)Excellency" or His Eminence. Also AS or (as) means "To Him Peace" (Peace Upon Him)"*

Muhammad al Baqir the Fourth or Fifth (Twelver) Imam said of the Mahdi: The Master of the Command was named as the Mahdi because he will dig out the Torah and other heavenly books from the cave in Antioch and judge among the people of the Torah according to the Torah; among the people of the Gospel according to the Gospel; among the people of the Psalms in accordance with the Psalms among the people of the Qur'an in accordance with the Qur'an.

Jafar al Sadiq, the Sixth Imam, made the following prophecies: Abu Bashir says: When I asked Imam Ja'far al-Sadiq, "O son of the Messenger of God! Who is the Mahdi of your clan ?", he replied: "The Mahdi will conquer the world; at that time the world will be illuminated by the light of God, and everywhere in which those other than God are worshiped will become places where God is worshiped; and even if the polytheists do not wish it, the only faith on that day will be the religion of God.

Sadir al-Sayrafi says: I heard from Imam Abu Abdullah Ja'far al-Sadiq that: Our modest Imam, to whom this occultation belongs [the Mahdi], who is deprived of and denied his rights, will move among them and wander through their markets and walk where they walk, but they will not recognize him

Abu Bashir says: I heard Imam Muhammad al-Baqr say: "He said: When the Mahdi appears he will follow in the path of the Messenger of God. Only he [the Mahdi] can explain the works of the Messenger of God. The face of the Mahdi shall shine upon the surface of the Moon.

According to Moojan Momen, among the most commonly reported signs that presage the advent of the Mahdi in Shia Islam are the following:

- The vast majority of people who profess to be Muslim will be so only in name despite their practice of Islamic rites and it will be they who make war with the Mahdi.

- Before his coming will come the red death and the white death, killing two thirds of the world's population. The red death signifies violence and the white death is plague. One third of the. world's population will die from the red death and the other third from the white death.

- Several figures will appear: the one-eyed Antichrist (*Masih ad-Dajjal*), the Sofyani and the Yamani.

- There will be a great conflict in the land of Syria, until it is destroyed.

- Death and fear will afflict t

Hadiths on Mahdi

In order to fully understand the Qur'an and the origins of Islamic Shariah law, one must know that the majority of it is taken from the Hadith and not the Qur'an. Women for example have rights that are granted to them in the Qur'an which are subsequently interpreted away in the Sahih Muslim. To fully understand the Islamic concept of Messiah, you must study the Hadith more-so than the Qur'an. I have included a few of these traditions from the Hadith, which I found in Wikipedia

Linage of Mahdi-

The Messenger of Allah (peace be upon him and his family) has said: "Al-Mahdi is from my progeny; his face is like the brightly illuminated moon."

Biharul Anwar, Volume 51, Page 85; Kashful Ghammah

The City of Qum and the Helpers of the Imam

Imam Ja'far ibn Muhammad as-Sadiq (peace be upon them both) has said: "The city of Qum has been named so because its inhabitants will gather with the Qa'im from Ale Muhammad [lit. one who will rise up from the progeny of Muhammad] and will stand alongside him, will strive to be hold firm to (their belief and assistance) of him and will assist him."

Safinatul Bihar, Volume 2, Page 446

Women in the Imam's Army- Imam Ja'far ibn Muhammad as-Sadiq (peace be upon them both) has said: "There will be thirteen women alongside al-Qa'im [when he makes his advent]."

Al-Mufadhal [the narrator of this tradition] asked the Imam: "And what will their role be?" The Imam replied: "They will treat the injured and look after the sick just as the [women did] at the time of the Messenger of Allah [during the battles]."

Ithbatul Hudat, Volume 7, Page 150

The Most Beloved to the Prophet ('s) The Messenger of Allah (peace be upon him and his family) has said: "Congratulations to the person who meets the Qa'im [one who will rise] from my Ahlul Bayt and has firm belief in him before his advent. He will have love for his friends, and will distance himself from his enemies and will have love for the leaders of guidance (the Imams) who came before him. Indeed these are my true friends, those whom I have love and affection for and (they) are the noblest of people from my nation."

Biharul Anwar, Volume 52, Page 129; al-Ghaybah of Shaykh Tusi

Greeting Imam al-Mahdi

A man once asked Imam Ja'far ibn Muhammad as-Sadiq (peace be upon both of them) how he should send his salutations upon Imam al-Qa'im (may Allah hasten his advent) and the Imam replied:

"Say: Greetings be upon you, O' Remnants of Allah [As-Salamu 'Alaykum Ya Baqiyatullah]!"

Biharul Anwar, Volume 52, Page 373, Tafsir Furat ibn Ibrahim

Anticipate the Advent of the Imam

Imam Ja'far ibn Muhammad as-Sadiq (peace be upon both of them) said: " ... During that time (the period of the occultation), await the advent (of the Imam) every morning and evening ... " Usul al-Kafi, Volume 1, Page 323

When Will the Time Come?

The Messenger of Allah (peace be upon him and his family) has said: "The appointed time (of the Day of Resurrection) will not come until the one from among us (the Ahlul Bayt) will rise with the truth and make his advent [Imam al-Mahdi], and this will take place when Allah, the Noble and Grand permits. So whoever obeys him shall be saved, and whoever goes against him will be destroyed..." Wasa'il ash-Shi'a, Volume 7, Page 325, hadith 6

Prepare for the Imam

Imam Ja'far ibn Muhammad as-Sadiq (peace be upon both of them) said: "Each one of you must prepare (your weapons) for the advent of al-Qa'im (peace be upon him), even if it be (as little as) an arrow, because when Allah the High, knows that a person has this intention, then He will give him a longer life."

Biharul Anwar, Volume 52, Page 366; al-Ghaybah of al-Nu'mani

How to Die while on the Path of the Imam. Imam Ja'far ibn Muhammad as-Sadiq (peace be upon both of them) said: "The person from amongst you who dies while awaiting this command [the advent of Imam al-Mahdi] is like a person who was with al-Qa'im in his tent ... no rather, he would be like a person who was fighting along-side him with his sword ... no rather, by Allah, he would be like the person who attained martyrdom along-side the Messenger of Allah (peace be upon him and his family)."

Biharul Anwar, Volume 52, Page 126; al-Mahasin

The First Ranked Soldiers of the Imam Imam Muhammad ibn 'Ali al-Baqir (peace be upon both of them) said: " ... Indeed he (al-Mahdi) will come and I swear by Allah that there will be three hundred and ten and some odd number of men with him and among them there will be fifty women who will all gather together in Makkah (to help him) ... "

Biharul Anwar, Volume 52, Page 223; Tafsir of al-'Ayyashi

In addition to the two major branches of Islam, there is another, much smaller branch known as the **Ahmadiyya.** This sect arose in India during the British colonial period at the end of the nineteenth century. Thus by the historical standards of Islam, this sect is quite new. It originated with a man by the name of Mirza Ghulam Ahmad (835 – 1908). He claimed to be the promised world reformer of the end of days, spoken of in Islamic Prophecy and the prophecies of other religious traditions as well. Thus he claimed to be the messiah who was to herald the final triumph of Islam across the world. He claimed to be the Mujaddid (divine reformer) of the 14th century of Islam and the prophesied Mahdi. Here is a summary of Ahmadiyya concept of messiah, drawn from Wikipedia;

The beliefs of the Ahmadiyya are similar to the Sunnis but there are some key differences. They believe that the claims made by their founder were true and that he was commissioned by Allah as a true reflection of the prophet-hood of Mohammed, who was to establish the unity of Allah and to remind humanity of their duties and responsibilities towards Allah and his creation. The Ahmadiyya teach that Mirza Ghulam Ahmad was the representative and spiritual re-advent of Mohammed and all other prophets. Thus the Mahdi. Ahmadiyya Islam believes that the Christians are in error for believing that their Messiah was the Son of God and like other Muslims, believe that Isa was a mere Prophet, and in no way divine. They consider this to be an affront to the rights of Allah. They teach that because of this, according to Islamic eschatology, the promised reformer has been given the title, **"Mahdi".** This means that he is guided by Allah and is the heir to all truths and in whom the attribute of "guide" of Allah gains full and complete representation..

Ahmadiyya Islam does not believe in Jihad. Thus they are not sponsors of terrorists or groups of Mujahedin or Ghazis. They believe that Islam is to be spread by peaceful missionary and evangelism. They believe and teach that the rest of Islam has erred in regard to creation by unjustly raising the sword and calling it jihad. And misunderstand the concept and purpose of Jihad.

Their belief concerning Yeshua ha Notzri (Jesus of Nazareth) is that he is "**Isa Masih**" (Yeshua the Messiah) They teach that the term, "Masih" is in relation to his role in the re-establishment of the rights of Muslims, by reforming their distorted, violent notion of Holy War and to reform the hearts and attitudes of the Jewish People.

Below is a list of distinct Ahmadiyya beliefs which I found in Wikipedia;

In Islam Ahmadiyya, the terms "Messiah" and "Mahdi" are synonymous terms for one and the same person. Like the term Messiah which, among other meanings, in essence means being *anointed* by God or *appointed* by God the term "Mahdi" means *guided* by God, thus both imply a direct ordainment and a spiritual nurturing by God of a divinely chosen individual. According to Ahmadiyya thought, Messiahship is a phenomenon, through which a special emphasis is given on the transformation of a people by way of offering suffering for the sake of God instead of giving suffering (i.e. refraining from revenge). Ahmadi Muslims believe that this special emphasis was given through the person of Jesus and Mirza Ghulam Ahmad among others.

Ahmadi Muslims hold that the prophesied eschotological figures of various religions, the coming of the Messiah and Mahdi in fact were to be fulfilled in one person who was to represent all previous prophets. The prophecies concerning the Mahdi or the second coming of Jesus are seen by Ahmadis as metaphorical, in that one was to be born and rise within the dispensation of Muhammed who by virtue of his similarity and affinity with Jesus of Nazareth, and the similarity in nature, temperament and disposition of the people of Jesus' time and the people of the time of the promised one (the Mahdi) is called by the same name. As the beliefs of all Muslims seems to be fulfilled yet in one person. Numerous Hadith are presented by the Ahmadis in support of their view such as one from Sunan ibn Majah which says

> *There is no Mahdi but Jesus Son of Mary*
> Ibn Majahm Bab, Shahadatu Zaman

Although the central values of Islam (prayer, charity, fasting, etc.) and the six articals of belief of Ahmadis are identical to those of mainstream Sunni Muslims and central to Ahmadi belief,inct Ahmadiyya beliefs include the following:

- That the prophecies concerning the second coming of Jesus were metaphorical in nature and not literal because Jesus is in their belief dead, and that Mirza Ghulam Ahmad fulfilled in his person these prophecies and the second advent of Jesus, that he was the promised Mahdi and Messiah.

- The continuation of divine revelation. Although the Qur'an is the final message of God for mankind, he continues to communicate with his chosen individuals in the same way he is believed to have done in the past. All of God's attributes are eternal.

- That Jesus, contrary to mainstream Islamic belief, *was* crucified and survived the four hours on the cross. He was later revived from a swoon in the tomb Amadis believe that Jesus died in Kashmir of old age whilst seeking the Lost Tribes of Israel. Jesus' remains are believed to be entombed in Kashmir under the name Yuz Asaf. Ahmadis believe that Jesus foretold the coming of Muhammad after him, which Christians have misinterpreted.

- That the "Messiah" and the "Imam Mahdi" are the same person, and that it is through his teachings and influence and through his prayers and those of his followers that Islam will defeat the Anit-Christ or Dajjal in a period similar to the period of time it took for nascent Christianity to rise and that the Dajjal's power will slowly melt away like the melting of snow, heralding the final victory of Islam and the age od peace.

- That the history of religion is cyclic and is renewed every seven millennia. The present cycle from the time of the Biblical Adam is split into seven epochs or ages, parallel to the seven days of the week, with periods for light and darkness. Mirza Ghulam Ahmad appeared as the promised Messiah at the sixth epoch heralding the seventh and final age of mankind,] as a day in the estimation of God is like a thousand years of man's reckoning.[Qur'an 22:47] According to Ghulam Ahmad, just as the sixth day of the week is reserved for Juma'ah (congregational prayers), likewise his age is destined for a global assembling of mankind in which the world is to unite under one universal religion: Islam.

- The two Ahmadiyya groups have varying beliefs regarding the finality of the Prophethood of Muhammad. The Ahmadiyya Muslim Community believes that Muhammad brought prophethood to perfection and was the last law-bearing prophet and the apex of humankind's spiritual evolution. New prophets can come, but they must be completely subordinate to Muhammad and cannot exceed him in excellence nor alter his teaching or bring any new law or religion. They are also thought of as reflections of Muhammed rather than independently made into Prophets, like the Prophets of antiquity. The Lahore Ahmadiyya Movement believes that Muhammad is the last of the prophets and no prophet, new or old, can come after him, also rejecting any notion of Jesus returning to earth as a Prophet.

Ahmad is consider to be a heretic by the rest of Islam because of his peaceful beliefs and his attempts to reform the violence out of Islam. They consider Ahmad to be a false prophet. Since the founding of the movement in 1889, they have been subject to persecution and rejection by the other sects of Islam.. The courts of India supported the Ahmadiyyas in a landmark decision on December 8th 1970, upholding their status as Muslims and that the other Muslim sects could not declare them as apostates because they hold the same fundamental beliefs as do other Muslims: there is no god but Allah and Muhammad is his Prophet.

In April 1974, 140 delegations from all over the world met at the annual Muslim World League in Mecca, Saudi Arabia. The League issued the following proclamation:

Qadiannism or Ahmadiyyat: It is a subversive movement against Islam and the Muslim world, which falsely and deceitfully claims to be an Islamic sect; who under the guise of Islam and for the sake of mundane interests contrives and plans top damage the very foundations of Islam.

Ahmadiyyans are not consider Muslims in Pakistan and are denied their right to the annual pilgrimage to Mecca, *"Hajj,"* unless they conceal the fact that they are Ahmadiyyans when they apply for their visas into Saudi Arabia. This was this first major effort to reform Islam and take the violence out through the reinterpretation of the Qur'an and Hadith and we see the result.

So as we come to the conclusion of this section on Islamic Concepts of Messiah. I can say, that as a Messianic Jew, I am not fond of the Sunni and Shi'ite concepts of messiah. I prefer the Ahmadiyya concept over the other two because it is a peaceful concept that does not call for the murder of the Jewish people and does not seek conversion by the sword.. I do not care for the concept of a Crusading Mahdi, as all non-Muslims are slated for violent death under the decree of this Mahdi! Mahdi fever is on the rise across Iran, Iraq, and Lebanon. Our forces have had to do battle in Iraq with a force known as the Mahdi

Army, and in Lebanon, Israel had to battle against Hezbollah during the 2nd Lebanon War. That campaign was mishandled by the Olmert Government as thousands of rockets reigned down on Galilee. Since the supposed cease fire, the Hezbos have been rearmed by the Iranians in this mad quest to bring in the era of the Mahdi. Hezbollah means," **Army of Allah**," and are led by **Nasrallah,** who is a Persian Puppet. Hezbollah is nothing more than a heavy Iranian Infantry Division on the ground in Lebanon. And we don't leave Syria out of this. They are strong allies of Iran and a state sponsor of global terrorism.

The years 2011 and 2012 saw a series of uprisings across the Islamic world. The modern-day Pharaoh,Hosni Mubarak was swept from power and Egypt and has now fallen under the control of the Muslim Brotherhood. This is foreboding for Israel and the west. The rebellion in Syria continues as the Allawite Muslim Regime of Bashar Assad slaughters thousands in a mad attempt to hang on to power. Assad is a Muslim ruler that brings to mind the Islamic doctrine of the Sofyani. The civil war in Syria has served to curb the military moves against Israel by Iran, who have a strong Axis-of-Evil ally in the current Syrian regime. I fear that at the end of this affair, Syria will fall under an Islamo-Fascist regime which will thus be prepared for the arrival of the Mahdi.

The wicked regime of Muammar Gaddafi has been removed from power in Libya with the help of the western allies and the dictator is dead. However we see again the rise of militant Islam there, and Libya will be another Arab nation preparing for the arrival of the Mahdi. Changes are coming as well in Yemen and in other Arab states, and the people who believe strongly in this, await the arrival of the Mahdi and then the return of Isa. See appendix one for how Islam and the Mahdi are foretold in biblical prophecy.

Mochiach Ben Dovid

(Messiah Son of David)

Now we turn to traditional *Rabbinic Judaism*. What are their concepts of the messiah? This is a huge subject. Very hard to explain it in a very short format. However, I will make the attempt. The Christians have inherited their own concepts of messiah from the Torah and from the Jews' although the two groups differ in what they believe his nature to be. To Christians and Messianic Jews,the messiah is part of G-d, manifest in a physical embodiment. But to Rabbinic Judaism, the messiah is a heroic Holy Man, chosen by G-d to save Israel, restore the Temple, and to exhault Israel above all nations by crushing her enemies on a global scale, during the wars of Gog and Magog. He will then usher in an era of everlasting peace.

This concept of messiah, originates in the writings of the great prophets of Israel, beginning with *Moshe Rabbienu* (Moses our teacher) and continued on by the visions of *Yeshayahu* (Isaiah) *Yirmeyahu* (Jeremiah) *Yechizikel* (Ezekiel) *Daniel* and *Zakarya* (Zachariah) and many more. It is carried on in the writings of the Rabbis: The Mishna, Talmud, Midrash, and the Zohar. They are quite voluminous and so if one wants to enrich their lives by studying the Rabbinic literature, I have listed them in the appendixes at the end of this book,;

The first passage in the Torah that has been identified as Messianic is in Bereshith (Genesis)

> ADONAI, God, said to the serpent, "Because you have done this, you are cursed more than all livestock and wild animals. You will crawl on your belly and eat dust as long as you live. I will put animosity between you and the woman, and between your descendant and her descendant; he will bruise your head, and you will bruise his heel." [Bereshith (Genesis) Chapter 3: 14 – 15;]

This is in reference to Satan, who had deceived Havah (Eve) into sinning. The LORD G-d gave the first recorded Prophecy. He promised that a redeemer would come for mankind, by being born from the womb of a daughter of Havah. The redeemer would crush Satan's Kingdom. Then comes a Prophecy by Moshe Rabbaneui (Moses our Teacher) in D'varim

> 15 "ADONAI will raise up for you a prophet like me from among yourselves, from your own kinsmen. You are to pay attention to him. [D'varim (Deuteronomy) Chapter 18: 15]

From this we learn that a great Prophet, on the scale of a second Moses would arise from out of the Sons of Israel. This was only the beginning. The Psalms spoke of a redeemer to come as well as the Prophets of Israel. The nation was being crushed by external enemies and the people were the victims of political oppression by wicked Kings like Manasseh and Achav. Wicked kings and even a couple of witch-like queens, Isavel and Athaliah. This together with a distortion of the faith and the adoption of paganism by the rulers of both Hebrew Kingdoms, Judah and Israel, caused G-d to send the Prophets. "Repent!" was the cry. In their writings they spoke of a ruler to come, who would be a just and righteous king, like King David had been, only greater.

> Who is this, coming from Edom, from Botzrah with clothing stained crimson, so magnificently dressed, so stately in his great strength? "It is I, who speak victoriously, I, well able to save." Why is your apparel red, your clothes like someone treading a winepress? 3 "I have trodden the winepress alone; from the peoples, not one was with me. So I trod them in my anger, trampled them in my fury; so their lifeblood spurted out on my clothing, and I have stained all my garments; 4 for the day of vengeance that was in my heart and my year of redemption have come. 5 I looked, but there was no one to help, and I was appalled that no one upheld me. Therefore my own arm brought me salvation, and my own fury upheld me. 6 In my anger I trod down the peoples, made

them drunk with my fury, then poured out their lifeblood on the earth."[Yeshayahu (Isaiah) 63: 1- 6;]

This is obviously speaking of a great warrior, who destroys the enemies of Israel, and his garments are stained by their blood. The Prophet Zakarya spoke very much about this. His entire book is *mystical* and *esoteric*. His visions both disturb and reassure. He sees terrible wars in the time just before the arrival of the Messiah..

> Then ADONAI will go out and fight against those nations, fighting as on a day of battle. 4 On that day his feet will stand on the Mount of Olives, which lies to the east of Yerushalayim; and the Mount of Olives will be split in half from east to west, to make a huge valley. Half of the mountain will move toward the north, and half of it toward the south.[Zakarya 14: 3 – 4]

In verses 12 and 13, the Prophet spoke of a horror that he witnessed in his vision, of a terrifying weapon unleashed upon the gentile armies by the messiah, who has arrived to save Israel in its hour of greatest need. Even greater than the holocaust apparently.

ADONAI will strike all the peoples who made war against Yerushalayim with a plague in which their flesh rots away while they are standing on their feet, their eyes rot away in their sockets, and their tongues rot away in their mouths. When that day comes, there will be among them great panic, sent by ADONAI, so that everyone lays hands on his neighbor, who in turn attacks him. [Zakarya 14: 12 – 13]

When the messiah arrives, this enemy army is struck with what appears to be some sort of Nuclear strike. Neutron weapons? And then the survivors turn against each other in confusion. This sounds like the same war spoken about by Yehezqel (Ezekiel).I conclude this must be the Mahdi Army we spoke about in chapter 1

We see from this tiny sampling of scriptures, how the coming of the Messiah was foretold. But how did the idea of, *"The Anointed One"*, come about? This is goes back to the formation of the monarchy during the days of Shmuel (Samuel) the Prophet. Not everyone in the nation was in favor of this. But those that were, suggested that the twelve tribes of Israel felt the need of a king in order to unite the people in the face of aggressive military incursions by the Philistines, Amalekites, and Ammonites. 1st Samuel 10:1 recounts the anointing of the nation's first King, **Sha'ul Ben Kish.** The LORD G-d's blessing was placed upon the King, by the application of specially consecrated olive oil on his forehead, between his eyes, and a prayer of authority and blessing was prayed over the anointee. As an *'anointed one'* (Mochiach in Hebrew) each king, beginning with Sha'ul Ben Kish. (Saul) was to be the representative of G-d in ruling his people according to the Law of Torah.

The greatest figure is David. In spite of his human frailties and failures in regards to his own family, **Dovid Ben Yishai** (David son of Jesse) became the model of just and humble ruler. The prophets, especialy Yeshayahu developed the idea that if Israel fulfills her role of being truly loyal to the LORD G-d, all the universe will enjoy a new age of peace. Most all of the kings after David and Solomon were dismal and disappointing. With notable exceptions like Hezekeyahu (Hezekiah) and Yoshiyahu (Josiah), most of the kings of both Judah, the southern Kingdom, and Israel, the northern Kingdom, were dismal failures who brought political, economic, and moral disaster upon the Jewish people. So the hope developed among the Rabbis, from their interpretation of the sacred scriptures, for a ruler who would truly demonstrate the qualities of an anointed one. A just and truly righteous king, a human figure, who was truly grounded in the Torah. He would bring in a golden age of righteousness. It was also understood from the scriptures, and taught by the Pharisees that on the Day of the LORD, the righteous dead would be resurrected to paradise, and the evil to judgment. These ideas are very strongly brought forth by the Book of Enoch.

There have been many men in the history of the Jewish people who have claimed to be the messiah, but all were proven to be dismal failures The predominate *Yeshivot* (Religious Academies) in the days of **Yeshua Ha Notzri** (Jesus of Nazareth) did not believe that the messiah to come would be the son of G-d. Large portions of the Jewish people did have this understanding, but they were not in positions of power. There were many Cohenim (Priests) who had this understanding, but again, they were not able to exercise influence in the power structure and Temple Yeshivot

The Rabbis were so certain that the messiah, when he arrived, would set up a political kingdom, that they rejected the claim of the *Rebbe Yeshua*. The government of the nation at that time was a den of corruption as well as puppets of Rome. These politicians plotted the downfall of the *Rebbe Yeshua*, and handed him over to the Romans. It was they who crucified him. not the corporate body of the Jewish people.

Others arose, who proved to be false messiahs. **Shimon bar Kosiba,** (known as bar Kochba, son of a star) led Israel in the last tragic uprising against the Roman Empire. He freed Jerusalem from 132 to 135 C.E.. He was proclaimed by none other than the great, Rabbi Akiva, to be the messiah. The Messianic Jews who believed that the Rebbe Yeshua had been Messiah, rejected this and refused to fight the Romans along side of a false messiah. They were right and by 135, the rebels had been slaughtered by the Romans. From this point in time, we count the bitter exile of the Jewish people from our land, which lasted until the rebirth of Israel in 1948

Another false messiah was a Turkish Jew named **Shabbetai Zevi.** He was a mystic who drew much of his beliefs from the *Zohar*, a great work which he misinterpreted. He drew large numbers of Jews from across central and eastern Europe to his cause. He began to cause a stir in the Ottoman Empire with his talk of rebuilding the Jewish Kingdom at Jerusalem. However, Shabbetai Zevi was all talk and no action. He never made any real attempt to begin the process of resurrecting the Jewish Nation. His was a false *Kaballah,* not a true

Kaballah. In 1665 he was arrested in Istanbul and brought before the Sultan Mehmed IV.

All pretenses of Shabbetai Zevi being the messiah fell by the wayside. It was shown that he had no power over the Turkish Sultan, who knew how to handle this matter. Zevi was found guilty of sedition against the Ottoman Empire and sentenced to death. However, if Zevi would convert to Islam, he would be be pardoned. Zevi converted and was released. His whole movement collapsed, just as the Turks knew that it would. There were still a few of his most devoted Talmidim (disciples) who promptly converted to Islam themselves. With this, Zevi discredited the whole Jewish Mystical Tradition, and it was cast aside for over a century. The *Zohar* fell into disrepute because of Zevi and his *false* Kaballah.

There had been a teaching that two messiahs would have to come. This resulted as the sages, in their concept of messiah saw him as a mere man, could not reconcile the many passages of the scriptures which spoke of a suffering servant. The dual messiah doctrine taught that there would be a suffering servant, known as **Mochiach ben Yosef**. He would come if Israel were not found worthy to receive the conquering King, **Mochiach ben Dovid**. Many saw Yeshua Ha Notzri in this role. If Israel were found worthy at the time that the messiah was due to arrive, Mochiach ben Dovid,(Messiah son of David) would come and usher in the golden age. Because they believed that the messiah was only to be a glorified human, they couldn't conceive of the idea that it would be the same messiah, coming twice. The first time as **Messiah son of Joseph,** suffering servant, and in the distant future, returning as **Messiah son of David.** This is exactly what the Messianic Jews of then, and now believe, as well as the Christians. As a result they have a different concept of messiah than does traditional Judaism. Today, all over the world, traditional Jews pray daily for the coming of the Messiah Son of David. The idea of Messiah son of Joesph is no longer taught by the mainstream Rabbis, because it naturally leads Jews toward Yeshua Ha Notzri, and into Messianic Judaism.

This is anathema to them, especially the *Gur Hasidim*, who persecute Messianic Jews, calling us soul thieves.

Traditional Judaism sees obedience to the Torah as a precondition that must be achieved before the coming of the messianic age. They pray for the messiah to come and restore Temple worship and sacrifices. Many non-orthodox Jews put the emphasis on a new age, a messianic age to come, instead of the actual coming of a physical messiah. They emphasize and pray for internal human transformation, instead of sacrifices in a new temple era. There are also those referred to as *Religious Zionists,* who strongly believe that in order to hasten the arrival of the messiah, they must reclaim and resettle Jewish people in our ancestral homeland in the mountains of Israel; the lands of *Judea* and *Shomeron* (Samaria), and on the Golan heights and in the Gaza Region. (The modern Philistia)

The scriptures teach that the Prophet Eliyahu (Elijah) must come first, to herald the arrival of Rabbi King Messiah. This specifically comes from the book of the Prophet Malaki

> 5 Look, I will send to you Eliyahu the prophet before the coming of the great and terrible Day of ADONAI. 6 He will turn the hearts of the fathers to the children and the hearts of the children to their fathers; otherwise I will come and strike the land with complete destruction." [Look, I will send to you Eliyahu the prophet before the coming of the great and terrible Day of ADONAI.[Malaki (Malachi), Chapter 4: 5-6]

The prophet Yeshayahu spoke also about a future herald of the Messiah, who is also identified as Eliyahu.

> 3 A voice cries out: "Clear a road through the desert for ADONAI! Level a highway in the 'Aravah for our God! 4 Let every valley be filled in, every mountain and hill lowered, the bumpy places made level and the crags become a plain. [Yeshayahu 40: 3 – 4]

Read the rest of this chapter and you will quickly realize that it is another Messianic Prophecy. But it is clear to the Rabbis that Eliyahu must first come. When the sages and even today's Rabbis are confronted with troubling questions that they cannot answer, they leave it to be answered by Eliyahu when he returns from *Gan Eden*. He will herald the Messianic age when all disputes will be resolved and true freedom and peace will reign supreme.

Talmud Bavli (Babylonian Talmud)

Now on into the Talmud. What does it have to say about the Messiah? To really understand what traditional Judaism believes in their concept of Messiah, you must go into the *Rabbinic literature.* As we have seen so far, all of this has been developed out of the Bible, but it is the *Talmud* and *Midrash* that which modern Judaism draws its doctrine and *halakot* (Jewish Law.)

There are hundreds of references in the Talmud concerning the Messiah, however only one seems to be skeptical about it. In the fourth century, Rabbi Hillel (not to be confused with the Hillel from the early 1st Century) declared, in tractate Sanhedrin, 98b;

> "Israel has no Messiah yet to come since he already enjoyed him in the days of Hezekeyahu"

He was taken to task for this doctrine but there seems to have been a substantial group who did believe that the Prophecies of Yeshayahu (Isaiah) concerning the Messiah had been fulfilled by King Hezekeyahu (Hezekiah). The Talmud was opposed to this idea and repudiates it in Sanhedrin 94a;

> Why has the word, lemarbeh, "the increase" (Yesh 9: 7) have a final Mem as a middle letter? The Holy One blessed be He, wished to make Hezekeyahu the Messiah and Sennacherib Gog and Magog, but the attribute of justice spoke before him, "King of the Universe! David, King of Israel, who composed so many songs and praises in thy honor, Thou has not made the Messiah, and wilt thou make Hezekeyahu the Messiah for whom Thou

has performed so many miracles and yet he did not compose one song for thee?

Look closely at this passage and it reveals what the Rabbis believe concerning the nature of the Messiah. It reveals their concept of Messiah to be one that holds him , not to be the Son of G-d, but a man who will be made into the messiah by Hashem (G-d) Now we go to Berachot 28b where we read about the farewell scene between Rabbi Yochanan ben Zakkai and his Talmidim. (Disciples) He gives them a strange, cryptic remark to them as he is laying on his deathbed:

"Prepare a seat for Hezekeyahu, King of Judah, who is coming."

We understand this to be a foreshadowing of the messiah, and if this is so, then this Sage of 1st

Century Israel identified him in some way with King Hezekeyahu. Rabbi Zakkai survived the fiery destruction of both Jerusalem and our beloved Temple. You already are beginning to see that there was quite a lot of debate amongst the Talmudic Sages, as to the identity of the Messiah. But all of them believed that it had been the LORD's plan, from the foundations of the earth at creation, to send the Messiah.

Though there was much speculation as to who the messiah was going to be, they all held the concept of Messiah, that he was just a divinely appoint human being, assigned this task by Hashem. Nothing more. It it is this idea that has left Israel open to all of those false Messiahs that we spoke about. Never does the Talmud assign divine or superhuman qualities to the redeemer, in its concept of Messiah. Where does the idea come from that he is to be from the lineage of King David? The Prophet Hosea declared in chapter 3: 4 – 5;

> For many days the children of Israel are to remain without King and without Prince, and without sacrifices and without pillar,and without shoulder garment or house idols. Afterward the children of Israel shall return,and seek Adonai their G-d, and David their King, and fear Adonai and his goodness in the latter days.

Look closely at this and your will discover, encrypted in these two verses major time periods of prophecy, and the things that must happen before the reign of Messiah.

1. *Destruction of the nation and end of National sovereignty for an unspecified length of time.*
2. *The return of the Jews to the land and the reestablishment of National sovereignty.*
3. *Spiritual revival and return to Torah.*
4. *Coming of Messiah*
5. *Complete repentance and salvation in the latter days.*

We can already see the beginning of the, Hosea process, coming to pass in the rebirth of Israel in the twentieth century, and the continued en-gathering of Jews. Then afterwords, the people will come back to the Torah. Then the Messiah will come and usher in the golden era. It is because of this verse and others like it, that the Hassidic Lubavitcher movement, evangelizes Jews the world over, trying to get them to return to all of the Torah Mitzvot. (Instructions) It is written

> "Afterward the children of Israel shall return and seek Adonai their G-d and David their king."

This is interpreted in Berachot 5a, as the Messiah;

> "The Rabbis declare, That is King Messiah. If he is born from among the living, David is his name.; and if he be from among the dead, David is his name."

But other passages of scripture establishes that the Messiah will not be King David himself returning, but that he will be of the house and lineage of King David. Tehillim (Psalms) 18: 50;

> "Making great the deliverance of his King, and showing kindness to his Messiah, to David and his seed, forever."

Notice that this is not referring to King David himself, but to his descendent. So from all this, we see how the prevailing belief was, and is, that the Messiah to come would be in the line of King David, and this is from where the common designation for him, 'the son of David' in Rabbinic literature comes from

Messiah's Name.

Now what about his name. The Talmud is full of debates amongst the sages as to what his name will be. I am just going to give a few small examples here. These come from several of the different *Yeshivot* (Religious Academies) of the Talmudic Rabbis. So it was that Biblical passages which have been interpreted as Messianic Prophecy, afford a variety of names by which the Messiah might be called. Some of the Talmidim of the Rabbis exercised their minds, in various ways of associating the name of the Messiah with that of their Rabbis. And indeed, this is not something that is confined to ages past. There were many in the Hassidic Chabad Lubavitcher Movement, that thought that their beloved Master, Rebbe Menachem Mendel Shneerson was the Messiah. He was a dear, sweet, and humble man, and after he passed away, many Lubatvitchers waited by his grave for a resurrection What is his name? The Yeshiva of Rav Sheila said;

"Shiloh, as it is written, 'Until Shiloh come' (Gen 49:10)

The Yeshiva of Rav Yannai declared;

> "Yinnon, as it is said, 'His name shall be continued as long as the sun. (Psalm 72:17)

The Yeshiva of Rav Channina declared;

"Chaninah, as it is said, 'I will show you no favor (Jer 16:13)

More is given in the following quote from Talmud Bavli, tractate Sanhedrin 98b;

> The Rabbis maintain that his name is 'the leprous one of the School of Rabbi Judah the Prince," as it is said "Surely he hath born our griefs, and carried our sorrows; yet we did esteem him stricken, smitten of G-d, and afflicted" (Is 53:4) Rav declared, The

Holy One, blessed be He, will hereafter raise up for Israel another David, as it is said, "They shall serve the LORD their G-d and David their King, whom I will raise up unto them" (Jer 30:9) It is not stated, "has raised" but "will raise.

Again is the following from Berachot 5a

> Rabbi Yehoshua ben Levi said, His name is Tzemach(the branch Zech 4:12) Rabbi Yudan said, It is Menachem. Rabbi Aibu said two are identical since the numerical value of the letters is the same.

In Tractate Sanhedrin 96b, Talmud Bavli, this exchange occurs;

> Rabbi Nachman asked Rabbi Yitzaak, "Have you heard when Bar Naphle (son of the fallen) will come?" He said to him, "Who is Bar Naphle?" He answered, "The Messiah" The other asked, "Do you call the Messiah Bar Naphle?" He replied, "I do, because it is written, 'In that day will I raise up the tabernacle of David that is fallen (Amoz 9:11)

The Rabbis found in the scriptures which speak of the coming of the Messiah, many attributes of his future mission. This gave rise to the debate as to what his name would be. More will be said about all of this when we get into the Messianic Jewish Concept of Messiah, regarding the name *Yeshua*, meaning *salvation*. Such a name is as appropriate as any of the other suggestions made by the Rabbis.

The Rabbis taught the people a doctrine called, **"Travail of the Messiah."** This teaches that in the days just prior to the arrival of the Messiah, that there will be pangs of suffering like as to a woman in childbirth. They taught, (on the principle that the night is darkest just before dawn), that conditions in the world just before the arrival of the Messiah would be a time of terrible tribulation and darkness. (The same thing taught by Yeshua) This in order to give hope and comfort to our people in times of terrible war and persecution. Tractate Sanhedrin relates how the youth will insult and turn against their elders and that the Beit Midrashim (Houses of Study) would be turned into brothels

There were many attempts in the Talmud Bavli to calculate the end times and the coming of the Messiah, and all of these proved to be wrong. It does speak of a seven year period of travail, just before the coming of the Messiah in *Sanhedrin 97a*. It speaks of the time of his arrival as one which is marked by political unrest, ending in bitter warfare. Strife symbolized under the term, *'Wars of Gog and Magog*. The Talmud of course draws all of this from the Bible. From Zakaryah, Dani'el, and especially the great work of the Prophet Yehezqel.(Ezekiel) But like all the modern day attempts to predict the **"Day of The LORD"**, it all failed. Most of the Talmudic predictions declared that it would be sometime in the fifth century of the common era. All this fell apart, and so the sages discouraged such attempts. Modern Judaism for the most part ignores the subject, leaving it to Christian Evangelicals to contemplate. Just like those in the Talmud, these Evangelicals have proven just as dismally wrong. Attempts to decipher the end of days and the time of the coming of the Messiah, are deprecated by most Rabbis , then and now, on the grounds that it raises hopes which are ultimately falsified.

All of this stems from the Jewish people's hopes being raised by men like the *Zealots* whose leaders in the late 2nd Temple period, sought to force the hand of G-d by taking up the sword. This resulted in the destruction of the Temple. Calamities are brought on by the likes of Shimon Bar Kosiba, Shabbetai Zevi, Reverend Jim Jones and many other false Messiah types! The Talmud itself, after recording all the past attempts and seeing them fail, brought heaps of condemnation on the practice. Talmud Bavli, Tractate Sanhedrin 97b;

> Cursed be they who calculate "the end," because they argue that since 'the end " has arrived and the Messiah has not come, he never will come; but wait for him, as it is said, "Though the appointed time tarry, wait for it" (Hab. 2:3)'

Another doctrine arose which taught that the date was not one that was fixed in time, but was affected by the conduct of the people of Israel. The reason the Chabad-Lubavitch movement seeks to bring all of the Jews in the world back to the ways of Torah is to hasten the coming of the Mochiach (Messiah) This thought was read into the words; Sanhedrin 98a;

> I the LORD will hasten it in its time' (Is 60:22) 'If you are worthy I will hasten it; if you are not worthy it will be in its time'

Here are several more statements from the Talmud Bavli which confirm this belief;

> Great is repentance because it brings the redemption near' (Yoma 86b)'All "the ends" have passed and the Messiah has not come; it depends only upon repentance and good deeds'.(Sanhedrin 97b) If Israel repented a single day, immediately would the son of David come. If Israel observed a single Sabbath properly, immediately would the son of David come' (Taanith 64a) 'If Israel were to keep two Sabbaths according to the Torah, they would be redeemed forthwith' (Shabbat 118b)

What kind of world will we live in when the Messiah rules and reigns on earth? The Talmud speaks of a time when the productivity of nature will be increased to a marvelous degree, and women will have painless childbirth. The effects that the reign of Mochiach ben Dovid will have upon the world is contained in the following material:

Ten things will the Holy One, blessed be He, renew in the hereafter:

(1) He will illumine the world; as it is said, "the sun shall be no more thy light by day, neither for brightness shall the moon give light unto thee; but the Lo0rd shall be unto thee an everlasting light (is lx 19) Is then man able to gaze upon the Holy One, blessed be He? But what will he do to the sun? He will illumine it with 49 parts of light, as is said, "the light of the moon shall be as the light of the sun and the light of the sun shall be seven-fold the light of seven days". Even when a person is ill, the Holy One, blessed be He, will order the sun to bring him healing; as it is said, "Unto you that fear my name shall the sun of righteousness arise with healing in his wings" (Mal. 4:2)

(2) He will cause running water to issue from Jerusalem, and whoever has an ailment will find healing there; as is said, "Everything shall live whither soever the river cometh.(Ez 47:9)

(3) He will cause trees to produce their fruit every month and all persons will eat of them and be healed; as it is said, "It shall bring forth new fruit every month...and the fruit thereof shall be for food, and the leaf for healing.

(4) All ruined cities will be rebuilt He, renew in the Hereafter: (1) He will illuminate the world; as is said, "The sun shall be no more thy light by day, neither for brightness shall the moon give light unto thee; but the LORD shall be unto thee an everlasting light"(Is 60:19) Is then, man able to gaze upon the Holy One, blessed be He? But what will he do to the sun? He will illuminate it with forty-nine parts of light; as it is said, "The light of the moon shall be as the light of the sun, and the light of the sun shall be sevenfold the light of seven days. Even when a person is ill, the Holy One, blessed be He, will order the sun to bring him healing as it is said, "Unto you that fear my and no waste places will remain in the world. Even Sodom and Gomorrah will be rebuilt in the hereafter; as it is said "Thy sisters Sodom and her daughters shall return to their former estate.

(5) He will rebuild Jerusalem with sapphires; as it is said, "I will lay thy foundations with sapphires

(Is 54:11) and, "I will make thy pinnacles of rubies" and those stones will shine like the sun so that idolaters will come and look upon the glory of Israel, as it is said "Nations shall come to thy light."

(6) Peace will reign throughout nature, as it is said , "The cow and the bear shall feed together.

(7) He will assemble all beasts and birds, and reptiles, and make a covenant between them and all Israel; as it is said, "In that day will I make a covenant for them with the beasts of the field" (Hosea 2:18)

(8) Weeping and wailing will cease in the world; as it is said, "The voice of weeping shall be no more heard in her" (Is 65: 19)

(9) Death will cease in the world; as it is said, "He hath swallowed up death forever,(Is 25:8)" (10) There will be no more sighing, groaning, or anguish, but all will be happy; as it is said, "The ransomed of the LORD shall return and come with singing to Zion."(Is 25:10.

We can very well see, that when the Messiah comes, he is to usher in a time of abiding peace and an age when the knowledge of the LORD will fill the earth, just as water fills the sea. I think it has all been well said, and to add more to it would be redundant.

There is one final item that I want to bring to bear in this section. It is the fact, that included within the teaching concerning the rebuilding of the city of Jerusalem, is the reestablishment of the Temple. This is the one that is described in much detail in the book of Yehezqel (Ezekiel). The Talmud teaches that our Temple as well as the city of Jerusalem were destroyed because of the iniquity of our people,. Today we can see that the State of Israel has succeeded in turning Jerusalem into a grand modern city. This is on a scale that the ancient ones could scarcely imagine. This restoration is all in spite of the fact that the bigoted Palestinian Arabs would rather see it all burned down, rather than it be under Jewish sovereignty. But what the sages wrote about was a spiritual concept, not the current Sate of Israel. Their concept was one where the Messiah would bring a sinless Paradise to Jerusalem. This is not humanly possible. I believe that this is a glaring contradiction to the doctrine, that the Messiah is just a mere mortal. No mortal can do all of these things. Only G-d can. More on this later As to the Temple, I have chosen this passage. It again illustrates that it is G-d who rebuilds the Temple. Even here in the Rabbinic writings, the line is becoming blurry between Hashem and the Messiah, even though the Rabbis still insist that Mochiach ben Dovid is a mere mortal.

> The Holy One, blessed be He, said, "I am He that made the Temple into a heap of ruins in this world, and I am He that will make it a thing of beauty in the world to come...He will rebuild the Temple and cause his Shekinah to abide there.(Midrash to Cant. iv. 4)

The Beit Ha Mikdash (Temple) has a different role to play in the Messianic Era, for sin has been eliminated. There will be no need for the sin offerings. But one sacrifice will be necessary, due to the feeling of gratitude which will fill the hearts of mankind;

> In the hereafter all offerings will cease except the thanksgiving offering which will never come to an end. (Pesikta 79a)

Do a study of the Great Temple described in the book of Yehezqel, starting in chapter 40. Then compare it's features to those of the previous structures. You will see that there are key differences. A good study of the Temple will yield rich rewards to you in your understanding of these concepts of Messiah. One final note, the Rabbinic writings teach that the wicked are excluded from the hereafter and are confined to Gehenna. If you are a Christian reading this, does it surprise you to learn that most of what you thought to be exclusively New Testament doctrines regarding the Messianic Era and the New Jerusalem, are core elements of Judaism. The only difference is that they did not recognize Yeshua (Jesus) as the promised Messiah, because their concept of the nature of the being of the Messiah is different from that in Christianity and in Messianic Judaism.

Mochiach Ben Elohim.
(Messiah Son of G-d)

For the next concept of messiah, we move into another form of Judaism. **Messianic Judaism**. Messianic Jews believe that Yeshua ha Notzri (Jesus of Nazareth) is the fulfillment of all of the Messianic prophecies that we were dealing with in the last chapter. Messianic Judaism teaches about both *Mochiach ben Dovid,* and *Mochiach ben Yosef.* However, they are **one and the same.** Thus, there are not two messiah's, each coming once,but one messiah coming twice.

The great Messianic Jewish sage, and pharisee, *Rav Sha'ul of Tarsus* (Apostle Paul), who studied at the Temple, in the Yeshiva (Religious Academy) of Rabban Gamaliel the elder, heard a Bat-Kol (voice) from heaven, and saw a vision of Yeshua Ha Notzri while on his way to Damascus. He teaches this concept of Messiah, throughout all of his writings in intricate detail,as does the author of the book of Evrim (Hebrews).

Rav Sha'ul (Master Saul) who is also revered by the Christians as their Apostle Paul, was born into a wealthy Jewish family in the land of Cilicia, in the city of Tarsus, in what is now southern Turkey. He was born a Roman Citizen, and his Latin Name was *Saul Paulus.* (This has been anglicized into the name, Paul.) From here, as a young man, he was sent to Jerusalem to become a Pharisee of the School of Hillel. His Rabbi was the aforementioned Gamaliel and under him Sha'ul became a Torah scholar par excellence. Rav Sha'ul had all the understanding of the concept of messiah that we discussed in the last chapter. He received authority, *S'mikah,* as a Rabbi, and rose in power and authority. I believe that he held a seat on the Great Sanhedrin, and was one of those that had Yeshua Ha Notzri, handed over to the Romans and crucified. He wielded police power and led the Temple Guards to arrest the Messianic Jews. He sincerely believed that what he was doing was for G-d, the same as do the modern orthodox *Heredi* and the *Gur Hasidim* who torment and persecute modern Messianic Jews in Israel. I am certain, that if one were to make a movie, where all of these events were taking place now in the 21st century, you would cast Rav Sha'ul as a Gur Hasidic Rabbi

The writings of Rav Sha'ul are very deep and come from a very esoteric interpretation of Biblical Judaism. Those that do not understand this context, and the Jewish culture in which they were written, are the cause of the misinterpretations that have arisen since the third century of the common era... So much so that translators brought much corruption to the basic understanding of Rav Sha'ul's writings. They teach that Rav Sha'ul converted from Judaism and taught against the Torah. To the Jewish people, he has become unrecognizable. How sad! In the last one hundred years, and especialy in the last forty years, this has been changing. Modern Messianic Judaism has begun to reclaim our ancient sage, and bring him back to the Jewish people, showing him to be a great sage and a mighty Pharisee.

Messianic Judaism now exists to be a bridge between traditional Judaism, and Gentile Christianity. A bridge across a chasm. A rift which developed between synagogue and church. Messianic Jews were expelled from the synagogue as *Minim* (heretics), because of our concept of messiah even though the Messianic Jews remained faithful to our people and to the traditions of the fathers, as well as to the Torah. So, it was that our ancestors began to meet in homes and then to found their own synagogues. They knew that G-d had called righteous Gentiles to the faith of the Torah and the holy and sacred traditions of the Bible, because of Yeshua the Messiah. Only later, when the Greek and Roman converts to Messianic Judaism outnumbered native born Jews, came unrighteous, unsaved Gentiles into the House of Yeshua.(Bet Yeshua.) A new name was given to them by Rome as a derision. "Christians."

The messiah, in order to do the things that he does, is much more than a mortal human being. No mere man or superhuman prophet can do these things. How many outstanding Prophets have arisen in history? Many. None of them have accomplished the deeds that the messiah is prophesied to achieve. These were men who called for a return to Torah, as instructed by Hashem, and many were cut down and persecuted by the government and religious establishment of their times. None of these Nevi'm (Prophets) were able to bring about the changes that were needed. Thus, no prophet born of mortality can be the messiah

Sin.

Let us begin with sin. Before the fall of man, Adam and Havah were clothed in radiant light. They experienced G-d in way that none of us today can fathom. They could see into the realm of eternity to that place beyond the mere physical. They could speak with their minds and hear each others thoughts,as well as those of angels and spirits. G-d spoke into their minds and they heard His voice. Humans are a hybrid species which combines a *spirit*, with that of a *physical being*. With sin, that which we call, **"The Fall of Man,"** was literally a fall from the true spiritual reality of creation, into the wholly physical realm of the animals which G-d had created. Our brain function was reduced to ten percent, lest we reach out with our sinful thoughts and destroy each other physically with telepathic power. We lost the garments of light and ceased to be radiant. We became naked flesh and very weak. So it was that Adam and Havah wrapped themselves in plant leaves and entered into dark depression. They cried out in despair, and after G-d had pronounced judgment, he had compassion on them. He killed a lamb, shedding its innocent blood, in order that the naked would be clothed.

This introduced the concept of blood atonement and covering for sin that an innocent animal had shed blood for the guilty. An ugly thing indeed! G-d wanted us to know how very ugly it is. Purity stained by blood and the stench of death. The Ancient of Days,blessed be His Name, illustrates how sin fowled up this universe at the time of the fall by the law of decay. This law of death, was introduced at that time because of sin. This is known in science as the second law of thermodynamics.

2nd law of thermodynamics: Physicist Lord Kelvin stated it technically as follows: "There is no natural process the only result of which is to cool a heat reservoir and do external work." In more understandable terms, this law observes the fact that the useable energy in the universe is becoming less and less. Ultimately there would be no available energy left. Stemming from this fact we find that the most probable state for any natural system is one of disorder. All natural systems degenerate when left to themselves

This is what the *Zohar* means when it teaches that all of this evil and corruption are a function of this universe, just like the law of gravity, quantum physics and nuclear string theory. For all of you who ask: Where was G-d in the holocaust? Why the killing fields of Cambodia? Why does G-d allow the murdering Jihadists of Islam? This is the reason. The law of decay is a function of this universe and that is way G-d instructs us in the ways of Tikkun Olam: Repairing the world. All of this is found in scripture

G-d is about doing the business of *Tikkun Olam*. That is why he began from the start, to establish a set of rules and a moral code. This was so that his people would be able to function and to have purpose to share in tikkun olam, made necessary because the law of decay had become operational in our universe. However, our efforts at Tikkun Olam are more for our own benefit and that of our fellow man, rather than a permanent fix. G-d himself wanted, out of his love and compassion, to fix the problem, rather than just wiping the slate clean, and blinking creation out of existence. Also, since the Ancient Holy One, blessed be His Name, is the author of all freedom, He wanted a way of Tikkun Olam, which would allow us a free choice. The Creator had not intended any of the sentient life forms that He created, to be bio-computers running a downloaded, *"Love G-d software."* The first messianic prophecy in the Torah was uttered by G-d Himself when He pronounced judgment on Lucifer. Then with the slaying of the first lamb at *Gan Eden,* the rule of blood atonement, sacrifice and covering came into effect

We are going to be covering a lot of material in establishing the nature of the messiah in Messianic Judaism. I want to show this from the pages of the Jewish Scriptures. I want to use strictly the pages of the Tanakh (Old Testament) to do this. For it was from these sacred writings that all believers in the coming or return of the messiah, draw their original messianic concept. This was well before the compilation of the B'rit ha dashah (New Testament) or for that matter, the Targums, Mishna, and the Talmud. In doing all of this, we will continue to develop the theme of blood atonement, and vicarious atonement. Without discussion of the covenants which G-d established, none of the material about the Messianic Jewish concept of messiah will make any sense at all.

I shall start with the first Messianic Prophecy, which can be found in the opening passages of the Torah. In B'reshite (Genesis) chapter 3. In this passage, G-d Himself is pronouncing judgment upon Lucifer, (ha Satan-the adversary, Satan'el, the Devil) and mankind. Starting in verse 14;

> And the LORD G-d said to the serpent "Because you have done this, you are cursed more than all livestock and more than every beast of the field. On your belly you are to go, and eat dust all the days of your life. And I will put enmity between you and the woman, and between your seed and her seed. He shall crush your head, and you shall crush his heal."

This is a curious and rather cryptic passage of scripture. The serpent is Lucifer, leader of the Evil Spirits and fallen Angels, who were already in rebellion against the *Eternal Order of the One G-d.* He is cursed over all creation. It states here that he will have an end, for it reads, *"all the days of your life"*. That implies that his life is not eternal in the physical sense, and that it indeed will come to an end. Next it states, that there will be war and struggle, between Satan and Havah, and then between Satan himself, and the offspring of the woman. Why did it not say, *"seed of the man"*? After all, it is the seed of a man, which inters into a woman to fertilize the the egg in the womb and produce a new human life. Instead it says. **"seed of the woman."** Women do not produce seed, nor can a woman become pregnant without a man. So this implies that in the future, a woman would bring forth a child in virginity and that this child would be struck in the foot by this deadly serpent. However, instead of suffering a mortal wound, this child would strike back, and stomp on the head of the serpent, destroying him.

So then the Torah goes on to describe in chapter 6 of B'reshite, a strange sequence of events. Angels, referred to as, *Ben Elohim*, (Sons of G-d) descend to earth and seize beautiful woman. These Satanic beings assume physical form, rape the woman, and produce a race of evil hybrids. These were called, *Nefilim* and were giants. Memory of these events are recalled in the stories of Greek mythology the *Titans* and *Hercules* etc. *Apollo* is a fallen Angel. He is known in the Bible by the names, *Abbadan* and *Apolliyon*. Lucifer never participated personally in these events, but sent out Apollo and others to contaminate the human gene pool, as a way of thwarting prophecy. He failed. Noach, says the Torah, in B'reshite 6:9, part b,

" Noach was a righteous man, perfect in his generations."

This is referring not only to the fact that Noach was a good man who was true to G-d, but that his family were, *"perfect in his generations,"* showing that his lines were not contaminated with the genes of the Nefilim, the spawn of Wicked Angels. If one wants to pursue this more, read the Antiquities of the Jews by the 1st Century Jewish Historian, **Flavius Josephus**. Also read the **Book of Jubilees**. These are good. Ancient, non-biblical sources, which go into more details about the Nefilim. As a result G-d destroyed the entire human race except for the immediate family of Noach , and then cast the offending entities into the Abyss to await judgment at the end of days. He destroyed the entire surface of the planet and changed its geography!

G-d established the **Human Covenant** with *Adam*, when he created Earth and deeded it to him, and by that act, to all of us. This was the first covenant. the *Adamic Covenant*. Man broke it, but G-d kept it. He saved alive one family of all the sons and daughters of man, ordained a second covenant built upon the first. This is known as, *The Covenant of Noach*. The LORD G-d changed the weather and atmospheric patterns of earth, allowing for sunlight to refract in the clouds, creating what we call a *rainbow*. G-d used this as a a sign, along with the shedding of blood. It was sealed when Noach offered up sacrifices and burned offerings.

> And Noach built an altar to the LORD and took of every clean beast and every clean bird, and offered burnt offerings on the altar. And the LORD smelled a soothing fragrance, and the LORD said in his heart, "Never again shall I curse the ground because of man, although the inclination of man's heart is evil from his youth, and never again smite all living creatures, as I have done, as long as the earth remains, seed time and harvest, and cold and heat, and winter and summer and day and night shall not cease. [B'reshite (Genesis) chapter 8: 20-22]

Noachic Covenant

This is the second covenant, built upon the foundation of the first. All of these covenants, are built one upon the other. The easiest way to remember this principle, that one covenant does not annul or abrogate another, is to think of them as a structure. Specifically, a step pyramid like the one in Egypt at Saqqara. Each one forms the foundation for the one that follows it, upward in chronological order. With the Noachic Covenant, the continuance of the Adamic Covenant is assured, and that the line of the messiah remains pure, firm, and intact, The first Messianic Prophecy is assured of it's fulfillment, in spite of the flood. So it would seem, that from what we know so far, that the messiah is going to be a man, born of a miraculous birth, from the line of Adam and Havah (Eve) following down through the second father of humankind, Noach

Now here are some small insights regarding the scripture passage we have just read. It says, "and took of every clean beast and every clean bird." This means that the concept of clean and unclean, things meant for food and those not, were already known from the beginning, well before the revelation of the Torah at Sinai. It says; "and the LORD said in his heart." Is Hashem speaking here to himself? No. He is speaking here into the heart of Noach, in response to Noach's prayer that G-d spare the earth in the future from a similar disaster. Noach handed down all of this in oral tradition to his son Shem, who then passed it to his sons, on to Avraham, and thence to Moshe Rabbineui, who first wrote it in the Bible. It says, "as long as the earth remains." This is telling us that Adonai our G-d, has a set time in which this planet will exist. Then he will make a new earth. But until this time, all the seasons and weather patterns and climatic cycles will remain as they now are, until the set time of the end has come.

In B'reshite 9:8-17, Hashem lays down in greater detail, the conditions which He Himself will fulfill. It is an established fact that only G-d is capable of keeping a covenant; man is not, as we have already seen. The only thing required of man, was that we not drink blood, and we couldn't keep even that, one, simple, stipulation. The rest of it is on Hashem to fulfill.

"And ADONAI spoke to Noach and his sons with him saying. "And see I establish my covenant with you and with your seed after you, and with every living creature that is with you: of the birds, of the cattle, and of every beast of the earth with you, of all that go out of the ark,every beast of the earth. And I shall establish my covenant with you, and never again is all flesh cut off by the waters of the flood, and never again is there a flood to destroy the earth."And G-d said, "This is the sign of the covenant which I make between me and you, and every living creature that is with you, for all generations to come. I shall set my rainbow in the cloud, and it shall be for a sign of the covenant between me and the earth. And it shall be, when I bring a cloud over the earth, that the rainbow shall be seen in the cloud, and I shall remember My covenant which is between me and you and every living creature of all flesh, and never again let the waters become a flood to destroy all flesh. And the rainbow shall be in the cloud, and I shall see it, to remember the everlasting covenant between G-d and every living creature of all flesh that is on the earth. And G-d said to Noach, "This is the sign of the covenant which I have established between Me and all flesh that is on the earth."

Notice that it is G-d who established the promises here and put himself under his own law. For it is only He, the great *Keter*, or *Ein Sof*, both terms which mean, the unknowable part of G-d, that is able to keep a covenant. He is without sin and we are not. This shows that any messiah, even though coming from the womb of a woman, has to be far greater than a mere mortal. He must if he is going to crush the head of Satan! Satan was a Keruv (Cherib) before his downfall, and that is far greater than an Angel, or a Principality of the Air. We read in the book of the Prophet Yeshayahu (Isaiah) chapter 37 :36

And an Angel of ADONAI went out and killed in the camp of the Assyrians 185,000. And they arose early in the morning and saw all of them, dead bodies

This is one Angel! One Angel killed 185,000 Assyrian Army Troops! Satan is far greater in power than any angel. So how is it then, that a mere man, super prophet, military conqueror, etc, would be able to slay Satan. Only G-d could do that. So it seems that only G-d himself is capable of fulfilling the first Messianic Prophecy. But how can this be? Can G-d be born of a woman, which he himself had created? It sounds so wild and preposterous. But never put the almighty creator G-d into a box. For it says in the book of the Prophet Shemu'el Alef (1st Samuel) chapter 16: 7b

> "G-d sees not as man sees. For man looks at the eyes, while G-d sees into the heart."

All of those people who declare that G-d cannot do this, or that. or will not do something that they perceive as outside their concept of

G-d and messiah,place the LORD into a box and try to mold the unmoldable. This is one of my criticism of Rabbinic Judaism, and Christianity. I see all of this from a *Zoharic* or *mystical* lens, more than *halachic* (legal). These mysteries and the contemplation of them make life worth living. Hallelujah.!

Avrahamic Covenant

The next covenant is that of Avraham (Abraham). You have to know all of this, in order to have a complete understanding of who the messiah is,what his nature is, and who his people are. G-d had to choose which branch of mankind in which to fulfill the first Messianic Prophecy, so he chose the family of Shem. From all the Shemite tribes, the Ancient of Days, blessed be He, chose the family of *Eber*, or *Heber*. (From whence comes the name, Hebrew.) Of all the decedents of Eber, He chose the family of Terah, who was a *Sumerian*, of the city of Ur. This city is an archeological ruin now, in southern Iraq.

The Talmud relates how Avram was against the paganism, into which the children of Noach had descended into. Even against his father Terah. Avram smashed his father's household idols. The story is even related in the Talmud and Jewish tradition that King Nimrud cast Avram into a brick kiln, but G-d saved him from the flames.

Now the family moved north, up the Euphrates River, and dwelled in the city of Harran, which still exists in a modern form in south east Turkey. Terah had three sons. Avram, Nahor, and Haran. Of these three, Avram was chosen by the LORD G-d, because of his faith, his generosity, and his conviction that all the pagan gods were false. Avraham had faith that the one true G-d, was the G-d of his ancestors, Noach and Shem. Because he chose G-d, G-d chose him. It would be his line from which the messiah would be brought forth in due season.

Hashem spoke to Avram (Avraham) and said, (B'reshite 12:1-7)

> "Go yourself out of your land, from your relatives and from your father's house, to a land which I will show you. And I shall make

you a great nation, and bless you and make your name great, and you shall be a blessing! And I shall bless those who bless you, and curse him who curses you. And in you, all the clans of the earth shall be blessed." So Avram left as ADONAI had commanded him. And Lot went with him. And Avram was 75 years old when he set out from Harran. And Avram took Sarai his wife, and Lot his nephew, and all their possessions that they had gathered, and the people whom they had acquired in Harran, and they set out for the land of Kena'an. And Avram passed through the land to the place of She'kem, as far as the terebinth tree of Moreh. At that time the Kena-anites were in the land And ADONAI appeared to Avram and said, "To your seed I give this land." And he built there an altar to ADONAI, who had appeared to him.

Look again. G-d first chose the man from whom to bring forth a nation of people. Then he chose a homeland for those people. The promise of the land, by G-d, was sealed in blood when Avram built an altar and gave sacrifices. Sealed in blood, once again. But this was only the beginning of revelation to Avram. So far, G-d has been making all the promises, and all Avram had to do was to believe, have faith and listen. For indeed it was going to take a powerful faith for Avram to believe that he would be father to a nation. His wife, her whom he loved so deeply, was cursed with a barren womb. She was a reproach and a laughing stock of the women of the middle east. For a woman to be barren, even today in the Islamic culture of the very same nations, is believed to be a curse from G-d. But never put G-d into a box. He's too big to fit! Cannot the G-d who created the womb in the first place, make it fruitful? He can and he did. The messiah must come from this line. The entire nation of Israel is the result of a miracle birth, thus setting precedence for the future.

This leads right into the *Avrahamic Covenant*, the next step on the road to messiah and redemption. It too is a pact sealed in blood. Rabbi John Popp, of Beth Shalom Messianic Jewish Fellowship in the city of Coeur d' Alene, Idaho, taught a wonderful lesson on this covenant.

Concepts of Messiah

He stressed that this watershed event, was absolutely necessary, and was a precursor to the receiving of the full Torah at Mt Sinai 400 years later. Rabbi Popp calls this, "*The Burning Torah Torch.*"

B'reshite (Genesis) chapter 15: 1-18;

> After these events the word of ADONAI came to Avram in a vision saying, "Do not be afraid, Avram I am your shield, your reward is exceedingly great"And Avram said. "Master ADONAI, what would You give me, seeing I go childless, and the heir of my house is Eliezar of Damascus?" And Avram said, "See, you have given me no seed, and see, one born in my house is my heir!"And see, the word of ADONAI came to him saying,"This one is not your heir, but he who comes from your own body is your heir"And He brought him outside and said, "Look now towards the heavens, and count the stars if you are able to count them." And He said to him, "So are your seed" And he believed in ADONAI, and he reckoned it to him for righteousness. And He said said to him, "I am ADONAI, who brought you out of Ur of the Kaldeans,to give you this land to inherit it." And he said, "Master ADONAI, whereby do I know that I possess it?" And He said to him, "Bring Me a three-year -old heifer, and a three-year old female goat, and a three-year-old ram, and a turtledove, and a young pigeon" And he took all of these to Him and cut them in the middle,and placed each half opposite the other, but did not cut the birds. And the birds of prey came down on the carcasses, and Avram drove them away. And it came to be, when the sun was going down, and a deep sleep fell upon Avram, that see, a frightening great darkness fell upon him. And He said to Avram, "Know for certain that your seed are to be sojourners in a land that is not theirs,and shall serve them, and they shall afflict them for four hundred years. But the nation whom they serve I am going to judge, and afterward let them come out with great possessions." " Now as for you, you are to go to your fathers in peace, you are to be buried at a good old age. Then in the fourth generation they shall return here, for

the iniquity of the Amorites is not yet complete."And it came to be, when the sun went down and it was dark, that see, a smoking oven and a burning torch passed between those pieces. On the same day, ADONAI made a covenant with Avram, saying, "I have given this and to your seed, from the River of Egypt, to the great river, the River Euphrates..

For those who are unfamiliar with the way in which middle eastern contracts and treaties, were sealed during this time, all of this may seem a mystery. Here is one such way. After the terms of the agreement had been thoroughly negotiated, animal sacrifices were prepared. The animals were killed, and placed in such a manner, that the blood would flow down into the path between the carcasses. Then, both parties to the covenant, would walk together, through the blood, saying, "If I fail to keep the terms of this covenant, let that which has happened to these animals, happen to me." Of course, the animals had been sacrificed, and the parties to the covenant had asked that they themselves end up like these bloody carcasses, which had been split in half. The path between the carcasses can be called; The trail of blood.

This is the procedure. What then is wrong with this picture? Avram is in a deep sleep, seeing all of this in the visions of the night. It was all happening, but Avram was being shown it while in a dream-scape or trance. He couldn't move! It was only Hashem who walked the trail of blood. So it stands to reason, that if the agreement were broken, it required that Hashem be made a sacrifice! He walked the trail of blood himself, knowing that humans are incapable of self atonement.. Incredible! So now we see, that the nature of the messiah, and his work, have to be greater than anything that can ever be accomplished by any mere mortal. He not only has to slay Satan, but has to die as well. He must walk the trail of blood for the Sons of Avram. How can G-d die, if he is G-d? Don't put G-d into a box by saying he can't. Is there anything impossible for G-d?

A side note; The River of Egypt spoken of here, is not the Nile. It is what is known today as, *Wadi El Arish*. This was always recognized as the eastern border of Egypt. It was the British who shifted the boundary farther east, into Jewish land, during the colonial period. The border now, is an artificial line in the sand, instead of the natural border, a wadi, set up by G-d himself. The border will go back to where it is supposed to be, because Hashem is not slack concerning his promises. Even though he may not do things in the time-frame that we humans think he should, does not mean that ADONAI will not Fulfill his word.

The next chapter in the Torah, deals with the attempt by Sarai, to fulfill the promises of G-d by using the code of Hammurabi. *Hammurabi*, a successor to Nimrud, was the current King of *Babylonia* and *Sumer*, where Avram had immigrated from. This King is called, *Amraphel* in the Torah, and the story of his wars in the region of Sodom and Gomorrah are found in B'reshite chapter 14. G-d had delivered this alliance of eastern Kings into the hand of Avram, whose forces were small and weak by comparison. This set a precedent for Abram's children. Israel, when it is in G-d's will, smashes enemy armies! It sets a precedence for the messiah who is always in G-d's will, and will smash the armies of darkness. In that final war, between the *Sons of Light*, and the *Sons of Darkness*, spoken of in Prophecy, and in the scrolls of the Essenes, messiah will lead us to final victory! But how? If the messiah is more that what the Rabbis say he is, but yet he has to die, how can he then be the commander and King? How can he lead the *Sons of Light* against the *Sons of Darkness?* We shall see.

Hammurabi had assembled and standardized a code of laws for his Empire, which covered all of what is now Iraq. His capitol was located at the city of Babylon. He was a Sumerian, and his laws covered not only trade and criminal justice, but also family law as well. Under this code, if a woman was for some reason barren, she could arrange for her husband to sleep with a servant girl. The child that was born of this union, would belong to the barren wife. It was supposed to work out, that the maiden would be a surrogate mother, and then barren wife would then by contractual adoption, become the mother of the child, raising it as her own. This only works if the birth-mother is somehow removed from the picture, and the child reared not knowing the circumstances of his birth. The law code of Hammurabi was widely followed due to the economic, political, and military influence of the 1st Empire of Babylonia, and thus it is no surprise to find this standard being applied by Sarai, with the full consent of Avram.

B'reshite chapter 16 tells us how Sarai took her Egyptian servant girl, and gave her to Avram as a concubine. This was not how G-d had intended to continue the physical lineage of the messiah. Not through the manipulation of a young woman as a surrogate mother! G-d intended this by means of a miracle baby. A baby produced in a holy and sanctified marriage, by an aging couple, whom the world said had been cursed by the gods. From a woman long past menopause. In spite of all this G-d did use the birth of Ishmael to bless Avram with many descendents. For from Ishmael sprang forth the seven sheiks of Arabia. All of the Arabs of Saudi Arabia, Yemen, Oman, United Arab Emirates, Kuwait, Qatar, and Bahrain, are the sons of Ishmael. Even after the death of Sarai, by then called, **Sarah**, Avram, by then renamed by G-d, **Avraham**, would remarry. From his marriage to Keturah would emerge the Bedouin Arabs, through his sons Kedar and Midian. Avraham has indeed, millions of Arabs as his physical descendents. But alas, because Avraham and Sarah chose to, out of shear worry and desperation from decades of waiting, childless, arose a fowl curse on the face of the earth. Islam. The tribe of Kuraish around Mecca, which can trace their origins through oral tradition, all the way back to Ishmael, produced the false prophet, Mohammed, and the worship of Satan under the name of Allah. From this, will come the Mahdi, the false messiah we have already spoken of in chapter one. So it is, that Avraham is the physical father of both the true messiah, and the Anti-messiah.

In B'reshite chapter 17, Hashem again confirms the covenant, and there we find the names are changed. G-d honored both Avram and Sarai, by adding letters from his own sacred name, to their names. He added in the letter hey, thus changing the names to reflect their role in the divine plan which was beginning to unfold on the stage of history. The institution of circumcision was established by G-d, for the nation which would give birth to the messiah. To this very day, the Jewish people do as required by G-d. Boys are circumcised on the eighth day outside the womb. These same passages also require that gentiles coming into the covenant be circumcised as well. From this we learn that the messiah must also be circumcised. in the flesh of his foreskin because he is part of the Avrahamic covenant.

A quick summary so far. We know that the messiah has to slay Satan and be perfect in his generations. He cannot have the blood of the Nefilim. He must be of the racial stock of Shem. Then a son of Heber, and following in that line, a descendent of the Sumerian Avraham, and circumcised into the covenant of Avraham. Further he must be perfect and sinless, as he is obligated to walk the trail of blood, if the sons of Avraham break faith with the covenant. But there is much more.

Avraham and Sarah begat the promised miracle baby, and called his name, **Yitzaak,** which means, *laughter.* A few years later, Avraham was forced to send Hagar and Ishmael into exile. Many people have speculated about the reasons, and have come up with different answers. But the Torah said that the son of the bondwoman would not inherit with the son of the covenant. Some of the Rabbis say that Ishmael was molesting Yitzaak. But whatever the reasons Sarah had, Hashem stepped in. This was because Avraham refused to send his first Son, beloved Ishmael into exile. He was angry.

> And the matter was very evil in the eyes of Avraham because of his son. But G-d said to Avraham, "Let it not be evil in your eyes because of the boy and because of your female servant. Whatever

Sarah has said to you, listen to her voice, for in Yitzaak your seed is called" [B'reshite chapter 21: 11-12]

This adds more to who the messiah is, and who he cannot be. He has to be a son of Yitzaak, and not of Ishmael. He has to be an Hebrew, and not an Arab or a Muslim. This is another reason that we know that anyone coming as the Mahdi of Islam is a false messiah. The Mahdi, even if he manages to convince many Jews that he is Messiah Son of David, and uneducated Christianity that he is Jesus Christ, is not the messiah. Spiritually, non Arab Muslims are descendents of Sheikh Ishmael. The messiah cannot be a non Arab Muslim. Nor can he be any kind of an Arab, whether Muslim or Christian. He has to be a Jew. He has to be of the blood of Yitzaak, which means that he cannot be a Jew who is a descendent of Ger Tzaddikim, such as the Ashkenazim of Eastern Europe. A great many are the Chassidic Jews of today. These same orthodox Jews, who declare that Messianic Jews and Reform Jews aren't Jewish, are themselves the descendents of Khazar Turks, who converted to Judaism during the Mongol era in Russia and Ukraine. The messiah cannot be a son of any of these kinds of Jews. Even though they are fully Jewish in Religion, they are not the physical sons of Yitzaak and none of them can be messiah.. Ger Tzaddikim means, *"Righteous Converts."* These are gentiles who have become fully Jewish through conversion like Ruth of Moab

When Yitzaak was 37 years old, ADONAI ordered his father Avraham, to offer him up as a burned sacrifice on Mount Moriah. We always have been taught that this was a test for Avraham. Indeed it was but even more so for Yitzaak. He was not the little boy like we like to picture, but a young man who knew that he was the heir of the covenant. He could have easily resisted being placed on the altar. Both father and son knew that, in order for G-d to fulfill the covenant, Yitzaak would, if sacrificed, have to be resurrected. This event in Judaism is called the *"Akkedah"* (The Binding). This event is replete with lessons of loyalty, faith, and dedication. The reason for including it in this lesson, is to illustrate a continuing pattern regarding Prophecy and the messiah.

> And Yitzaak spoke to Avraham his father and said, "My father!" And he said, "Here I am my son" And he said, "See the fire and wood! But where is the lamb for the burnt offering? And Avraham said, "My son, G-d does provide for himself the lamb for the burnt offering" And the two of them went together [B'reshite chapter 22: 7-8]

Take a look at this. It can be interpreted to say that G-d is making himself a sacrificial lamb, meaning that the Ancient of Days himself was going to be made a sacrifice. Knowing what we now now about the trail of blood, it becomes obvious that this is a major reason for this whole strange event. G-d is setting up the model events concerning the concepts of vicarious atonement, that were to be recorded in the Bible. Here G-d is in effect, creating the Bible by establishing the facts through the stories which would later be written down for us. The next meaning is for that very moment. G-d would be the one to provide the ram for the offering. And he did. Both men passed the test of their faith, and grew spiritually greater, becoming the patriarchs we know them as today. At the moment of truth, Yitzaak was fulfilling a command which would later be written down by ADONAI himself as part of the Ten Commandments. Honor your father and your mother. At the moment of near sacrifice, as Avraham was about to cut his son's throat, an Angel put a stop to all of this, and G-d placed a ram in the thicket. G-d showed that he does not accept, condone, or demand, that we offer up human sacrifices. They would be useless, because a mere mortal cannot even die for his own sins. This is because of the fact that he has sin in the first place! Only that which is without defect can die for sins, and a mere mortal messiah cannot fit this bill.

Next we need to move forward to Yitzaak's illustrious grandson, Yosef (Joseph). He is a foreshadowing of the messiah and a type who models the national redemptive role of Israel by the messiah. He is rejected by all his brothers, and cast down into a pit. Like a grave. This models how the messiah would be rejected by his Jewish brethren. However one brother, Reuven, repented of this, and wanted to return him to their father Ya'ocov. But the others would have nothing of it and Yosef was taken away by gentiles, and sold into Egypt. He served Potiphar the Captain of Pharaoh's palace guard. He rejected adultery and being falsely accused of rape, was cast into prison. Still G-d was with him and had given him the spiritual gift of dream interpretation. Because of this, Yosef was able to interpret the Pharaoh's dreams concerning the coming famine. Yosef was smart and educated, and provided a solution and thus averted the disaster. It was then that he was placed into power as the Grand Vizier of the Egyptian Empire.

Grand Vizier Yosef was soon married to Azenath, daughter of the Egyptian High Priest of the Temple complex at On. She converted from her paganism, worshiping Hashem, the one true G-d in heaven above and earth below. Two sons were born. Ephraim and Manashe. It was at this time, that his brothers descend down to Egypt to purchase grain for their starving families. Yosef puts them to the test, in order to find out if their character has changed or not. But in the end, he embraces them for it is written;

> "Then Yosef said to his brothers, "Please come near to me." And when they came near, he said "I am Yosef your brother, whom you sold into Egypt. And now, do not be grieved nor displeased with yourselves because you sold me here, for G-d sent me before you to preserve life." [B'reshite chapter 45:4-5]

We see the wonderful forgiveness in the heart of the grieved Yosef, whose life prophesied the reaction of Israel to the first manifestation of the messiah. Him they persecuted and rejected. Tossed him into a grave-like pit. He was pulled from the pit by gentiles, and later rises to be their prince. His brothers, when they see Yosef, do not even have a clue who he is. They don't recognize their own brother, and fellow Hebrew, who by this time is shaved in both beard and hair, dressed in gentile clothing, and speaking a gentile language. It is then that Yosef reveals himself, and they weep and repent. This will be true of the messiah as well. For it was spoken by the prophet saying;

"And they shall look upon Me whom they pierced, and they shall mourn for him as one mourns for his only son. And they shall be in bitterness over him as a bitterness over the first-born.[Zakaryah, 12:10; b]

Now we know from the prophetic life of Yosef ben Ya'ocov, that the messiah was to be rejected by his fellow Hebrews. Persecuted, maltreated, scorned, rejected and despised. But that the messiah is to have the heart of forgiveness, and when he is revealed a second time to Israel, they will cry because of him. Bitterness and wailing, having realized, just like the elder brothers of Yosef, their terrible mistake. And the messiah will not take out vengeance on them. He will say, that is was meant. That he had been sent ahead so that many lives could be preserved. And he will embrace them, and all of Israel will be reconciled. He will embrace Israel saying, "Come. I am your brother Yeshua. I am Yeshua."

Now we have to talk about a sordid affair, involving Yosef's older brother, Yudah.(Judah) The story of this man is very important, for the LORD chose him, out of all of his brothers, to be the founder of the specific tribe of Israel, which would bring forth the messiah and much more. He was the father of the tribe of his namesake, which later became the Kingdom of Yehudah, or Judah. During the days of the Maccabees, the name becomes, Judea, and hence the word, Jew. Or, Yehudi, which means, man of Judah. From this comes the word, Yid, or Yiddish, which is a Germanic term, that arose out of the Jewish communities of Eastern Europe. The language of Yiddish is a form of Germanic Hebrew, just as Ladino is a form of Spanish Hebrew of the Sephardic communities of Spain. Yudah (Yehudah; Judah) is the father of all of this, and his very name means, "Praise" Now since the lose of the tribal distinctions, all Hebrews from all tribes are referred to as Jews. There are no distinctions between Israel and Jewish. The Jews are Israel and Israel are the Jews.

Why didn't all of these honors go to Ya'ocov's oldest son, Reuven? Because he was involved in a near incestuous affair with his Father's concubine, Bilhah, the mother of several of his brothers. His rights as firstborn and heir were forfeit. Next in line were Shimon and Levi. These two betrayed Ya'ocov's agreement with the city of Shekkem(modern day Nablus) which settled the outrage of the rape of their sister Dinah by the Crown Prince of that city. Shimon and Levi led warriors against the men of Shekkem, when they were weak from having been circumcised. These Canaanites agreed to convert to the true worship of ADONAI, and had undergone circumcision. Shimon and Levi also led the sons of Ya'ocov, (who by now had been renamed, Israel) in the betrayal and attempted murder of their brother Yosef. So they were rejected. The next in line was Yudah, who saved Yosef's life, and later gave an eloquent statement of repentance offering himself as a slave, in place of his little brother Benyamin. He offered to take the punishment, and atone for the sins of Benyamin, who had been charged by the Egyptian Grand Vizier (Yosef, but still unknown as Yosef to the brothers) of stealing his cup of divination. Yudah was chosen by G-d to found the royal house of Israel and to bring forth the physical body of the Messiah.

What of this sordid affair I spoke of? Read all the details in B'reshite chapter 38. Here is a summary. Yudah's firstborn, Er, was married to a young lady by the name of Tamar. For some reason, the LORD G-d struck him down and killed him. Next, Yudah's son Onan married Tamar, in order to perform the duties of Yibum (Leverite Marriage). The child that would result would be called by the name of the deceased brother. However Onan was also struck dead, and Yudah's last son was Shelah, who was a boy far to young for marriage. So Yudah instructed Tamar to wait until Shelah was of age. But when that time came, Yudah refused to allow the marriage. Therefore Tamar, veiled herself as a Canaanite whore, and seduced Yudah in order to conceive a child. The result was the birth of twins, Perets and Zerah. It is from Perets that we begin to trace the lineage of the Royal line and the messiah. You must know of the affair of Yudah and Tamar, if you are to understand why, generations later, when the time came for Israel to have its first King, that G-d did not go directly to Yishai (Jesse) of Bet Lechem (Bethlehem) making him King, Instead, Sha'ul ben Kish of the tribe of Benyamin was chosen, Why? . In the Torah, it is clearly spelled out, that a *mamzer,(bastard)* is not allowed the normal privileges due to one who is born in holy matrimony. Is G-d being cruel here? Heaven forbid no! G-d is not punishing innocent children! Let's read the scripture verse first, and then I will explain what the intent of the law is. It is written;

> No one of illegitimate birth does enter the assembly of ADONAI, even a tenth generation of his does not enter the assembly of ADONAI.[D'varim (Deuteronomy) chapter 23: 2]

G-d is holding us as adults, responsible for our actions. If we go out and live lives of promiscuity and sexual license, giving birth to children outside of the ideal setting of matrimony, we are to blame. The parents are at fault for the suffering and heartache of these children! Did the child sin? No! It is the man who sinned when he seduced a teenage girl and impregnated her, making her a single mom! It was the woman who slept with her male lover when her husband was away! G-d is telling us how serious he regards the welfare of these babies, that we as sinners, bring into the world outside of Torah guidelines!The fact is that it is the parent, whose adultery and fornication have created a child ,who is considered by society as a second class citizen. In these modern times, a good many American children are mamzers and G-d will hold our society to account for this!

How does this law apply to the line of Yudah and the messiah? The curse of ten generations had not run its fill course, when the people of Israel began crying to the Prophet Shemu'el for a King. G-d would give them what they wanted and still not violate his Torah. Instead of the first King being a man after G-d's own heart, Israel got a corrupt middle-eastern dictator! Sha'ul ben Kish. Only afterwords would G-d bring in *Dovid ben Yishai*, who was the eleventh generation from the mamzer, Perets. We got Sha'ul ben Kish, because we, like Avraham and Sarah, were impatient, not willing to wait on G-d's timetable. Let this be a lesson for us. We want the messiah to return soon. But let us not be so impatient for him to come, that instead of getting the one after G-d's own heart, we get an anti-messiah. A man, who like Sha'ul ben Kish, starts out as something wonderful and brilliant, but then degenerates into a devil!

We will soon come back to Dovid ben Yishai, but now we have to turn to the Sinai Covenant. This is the revelation of the Torah to the Greatest Prophet in history, Moshe Rabbaneui, known to Gentiles as, Moses. It was Moshe Rabbaneui (Moses our teacher) who recorded the history of man in the book of B'reshite, wrote the story of the Exodus, the history of the people of Israel as nomads in the deserts of Arabia, and most important of all, the very words of G-d, the Torah. The Torah is all of the instructions given for mankind by almighty G-d. It is here that another level is added to the pyramid of covenants. It is the fulfillment of all the promises that Hashem had made to Avraham, Yitzaak, and Ya'ocov. That they would be the forebears of a great nation. A nation of priests.

The messiah had to have a nation to be incarnated into, and in order for a people to be a nation, they need laws. This is one of the most important roles of the Torah. It is the genesis of all the legal and moral precepts which govern the people of Israel. All Prophetic and Rabbinic legislation is built upon the Torah. All of the rulings of the Mishpatim (Judges) of the bible stem from the use of the Sinai Law Code, as well as the rulings of the Mishnaic and Talmudic Rabbis of the period of 70 C.E. To about 800 C.E. Even the Zohar stems from the Torah, and without the Torah, there is no Israel.

There is not enough space in this short book to go into complete details about every sacrifice and every offering, and of all the Messianic symbolism embodied in the Mishkan (Tabernacle). For this reason, I am going to stick to a few of the ones which I consider to be the most important. The ones that you need to know, to understand the Messianic Jewish concept of messiah.

The first thing I want to bring out, is the bread of the Passover and the blood of the lamb. The story of the first Passover is found in the book of Exodus and I am sure that most of you who are reading this already know those details, so I will keep it brief. On the night before our people were to depart from Egypt, G-d had instructed the people through Moshe Rabbaneui to take an unblemished lamb. Each family was to take a lamb, sacrifice it, and then smear its blood on the lentil and doorposts of their homes. The Death Angel was being sent by ADONAI that night, to take the souls of all firstborn children in the Egyptian Empire into paradise. Is G-d here a killer of children? No! Again, it was the sins of the parents, and most directly, that of the Egyptian Government which brought this on. All of these children were taken peacefully into heaven by G-d. They went to sleep peacefully that fateful night, and awoke in paradise. Here they remain, learning the ultimate Torah from the Living G-d. The Zohar teaches that children who die learn music in a heavenly Yeshivah (Torah Academy) having never known sin

Was it just Egyptian children taken? No. There were Israelites who worshiped the false gods of Egypt which ADONAI had been judging. These did not do as Moshe instructed. These parents of Hebrew babies suffered the same heartache as did the parents of Egyptian babies. G-d is no respecter of status, and Israelites, just because they may have been born as such, are still held to the LORD's standards, just as all men are. We see here, an innocent lamb, shedding blood for the salvation of sinful people, both Jew and Gentile. There were Egyptians who worshiped the true G-d, and these Gentiles had also applied the lamb's blood to their doors. These people are part of what was known as the, "mixed multitude," as well as a throng of other Gentile slaves, Libyans, Nubians, and Cushites, who fled Egypt into Arabia, along with the Israelis. Here we can see the concept, that the Lamb's blood was not only for the salvation of the Israelis, but for Gentiles as well. **Vicarious atonement.** Another thing we see is innocent schoolchildren being taken, swept away because of the sins of the parents. The ultimate innocence. Those who are not accountable to

G-d yet for sin, were swept away in death, Look at what the Talmudic Rabbis of Babylonia had to say about this concept. In tractate

Shabbat 33b; of the Talmud Bavli (Babylonian Talmud)

> Rabbi Gorian said (according to others, Rabbi Yosef ben Shema'yah) 'When there are righteous ones a generation, the righteous are seized for the sins of that generation. When there are no righteous ones in the generation, schoolchildren are seized for the sin of that generation."

Even in Rabbinic Judaism, we find the concept embodied, of the innocent suffering for the guilty. We as Messianic Jews share this concept with our fellow Jews. We know from the Tanakh,(Old Testament) that the messiah, in addition to being a conquering King, must also at the same time make vicarious atonement.

Now to the bread of **Pesach***(Passover)* How does this come into play? Strange that simple unleavened matzah should have embodied in it a concept of messiah but it does. It is made without yeast or any leavening agent. Leaven is a symbol of sin in the scriptures. If the bread is to be a symbol of messiah, who is sinless, therefore the bread cannot be baked with yeast. This bread is also made with salt. All bread in the Mishkan was made with salt, which represents blood. Here we have coming into play a *covenant in salt*. Another way of sealing a covenant, is to share a meal and partake together of salt. So the entire Festival of Matzah, which lasts for seven days, is our sharing a a holy meal with G-d, in which he confirms with every bite his **Messianic Covenant** with us by the sharing of the salt. So let us all celebrate the Seder meal and the seven days of Matzah, every year, knowing how rich and how rewarding it is.

During the days of Matzah, there falls a one day special celebration known as **Yom Ha Bikkirim**, or the feast of **First Fruits**. (This is not to be confused with Shavuot, which modern Judaism sometimes refers to as ,"First-fruits.") A good description of it is found in the book of Vayikra;

And ADONAI spoke to Moshe saying, "Speak to the children of Israel, and you shall say to them,When you come into the land which I give you,and shall reap its harvest, then you shall bring a sheaf of the first-fruits of your harvest to the priest. And he shall wave the sheaf before ADONAI, for your acceptance. On the morrow after the Shabbat the priest waves it. And on that day when you wave the sheaf, you shall prepare a male lamb, one year old, a perfect one, as a burnt offering to ADONAI, and its grain offering: two-tenths of an ephah of fine flour mixed with oil, an offering made by fire to ADONAI, a sweet fragrance, and its drink offering: one-fourth of a hin of wine And you do not eat bread or roasted grain until the same day that you have brought an offering to your G-d – a law forever throughout your generations in all your dwellings"[Vayikra (Leviticus) chapter 23:9-14]

I am spending more time on *Yom Ha Bikkirim*, because it is to often neglected when people are talking about the messianic significance of the Passover season. There are three different feasts going on during this time of year, *Pesach, Hag Ha Matzot*, and *Yom Ha Bikkirim*, with the last two coinciding and overlapping. All three of these are referred to as the Passover Season.

During this time of year in Israel, the barley has started to come up really good. The green stalks of the plants are shooting up. New life is everywhere, and it is the first of these new plants which are to be taken to the Temple. The Aviv Barley. It is a sign that the farmer is dedicating the first rewards of his labor, back to the Almighty G-d, who has provided everything to the people for life. The seeds from which these sheaves were grown, had been planted in the earth back in the previous fall, had been, as it were, dead and buried. However from the dead-looking seeds, having been buried, now sprout forth new life in a form symbolic of resurrection. The whole spring is about new life and resurrection. A sacrifice was brought. Once again, and unblemished male sheep, a yearling of the flock. The pattern is still holding true. Vicarious atonement once again. But there is more.

Flour and olive oil. The same flour from which the Matzah is being made, and oil, followed by wine. Here we have first, the sacrificed lamb, which is as we have established, symbolizing the messiah. Then the flour, which symbolizes G-d's provision of earthly bread, and of heavenly bread, which is the messiah. Then we have the oil, which symbolizes the Ruach ha Kodesh (Holy Spirit) and the wine, which symbolizes blood. All of this is burned up as a sacrifice, but now since there are symbols of resurrection in the midst of the sacrifice, Yom Ha Bikkirim is showing us something very important. The messiah, being the bread of life, filled with the Holy Spirit, shall have his blood poured out and his body consumed, during the Passover season, yet shall rise again on Yom Ha Bikkirim as the First Fruits of the resurrection. Let us celebrate in Messianic Synagogues everywhere and every year, *Yom Ha Bikkirim,* in honor of the Messiah Yeshua. We cannot do those things which require a temple, but that should not stop us from at least gathering the symbols and teaching their meaning. This is how we celebrate the days of unleavened bread.

Can any of the above be true, if the messiah were just a mere mortal man. Not even a superhuman. could do any of this. Therefore the messiah is way beyond being a mere son of Adam. One final note about Yom Ha Bikkirim. It falls on the third day after the beginning of the Passover Season. It is not Easter. Easter is pagan, its origins being the worship of a demonic fertility goddess by the name of Ishtar. (Also known as Astarte.) Bunny rabbits mate prolifically and were used as the symbols in this cult, along with what is known as the *golden egg of Astarte.* The Roman Catholic Church is responsible for replacing Yom Ha Bikkirim with Easter. They even arranged the calender so that Easter never falls on the same day as First Fruits, and always on a Sunday. We as Messianic Jews, do not partake of this pagan festival, which Christianity is trying to paint as something about the messiah. They replaced the name of Ishtar with Jesus, removing the sexual orgies that Ishtar worshipers engaged in, and then connecting it to the resurrection.

Concepts of Messiah

The next symbol is the **Manna** which came out of heaven. The Ancient Holy One, blessed be He, used this to feed our people in the Arabian desert. Yes, the Arabian Desert. We know that the actual Mount Sinai spoken of in the Bible, is *Jebel Al Lawz*, which is in *Midian*. Midian is located in the northwestern corner of Saudi Arabia. The tribes of Israel did not spend forty years circling the Sinai Peninsula of Egypt. The Torah says that Moshe fled Egypt, and dwelt in Midian. Midian is not in Egypt but in Arabia. The Sinai Peninsula has always been regarded as part of Egypt. In the days of Moshe, there was a very significant Egyptian military presence on the Sinai Peninsula, due to the fact due to the copper mines in the southern tip. The mines are near where the Christians claim Mount Sinai to be. Moshe fled out of the Nile region of Egypt. He was a Royal Prince of Egypt, and had been supreme Army Commander. The officers in charge of the Sinai military garrisons would have recognized their former leader, and knowing that he was a wanted man, would have arrested him. No, Moshe went to Midian, and received the words of Hashem at Jebel Al Lawz.

Lawz? Indeed it is ironic that the Arabic name for Mount Sinai in Midian, sounds exactly like the word in English for the instructions of G-d. *Laws*. A mountain where the Laws were received is called Lawz! Amazing. Now I know that the name, Lawz, in Arabic, has some other meaning than what the English name, Laws, implies. I just find it to be an extremely interesting coincidence. Or is it a coincidence?

What has any of this to due with the manna? It puts the wondering Israelites out into the Nefud Desert of central Arabia, a place too hot for even a lizard! No grass for the livestock! No rain! Endless, trackless sand dunes under a 130 degree blistering heat in the summer. This is why the people, who were used to the green Nile Delta of Goshen, cried out ,"Did you bring us here to slay us with thirst?" Millions of people and livestock were totally dependent on the bread which came down from heaven. This manna is therefore a symbol of G-d's provision of the Messiah Yeshua, who is the spiritual bread which comes down from heaven. He sustains us with salvation as we travel through the Nefud Deserts of our lives. The bread of salvation. The living manna.

Next I will mention the Red Heifer. This rather strange procedure is found in B'midbar (Numbers) chapter 19, which is the beginning of *Parashah* 39: *Hukkat* (Regulation), in the yearly Torah reading cycle of all Jewish Synagogues, be they Messianic, Orthodox, or otherwise. This cow had to be completely rusty red, with no white hair, and without blemish. It was not sacrificed in the temple, but was taken outside the camp, and offered as a burned sacrifice. We do not have to have a Mishkan or a Temple to offer this. It was designed to impart ritual purity for those who had come into contact with a dead person. The ashes of the cow were then mixed with hyssop and cedar wood, and a piece of scarlet yarn, while still ablaze. These ashes were then mixed with water, which was applied to those priests who had incurred ritual impurity after contact with a corpse. Those who prepared the mixture were then ritually unclean until the evening. Another Cohen (Priest) who had not incurred ritual impurity, would collect the mixture and store it outside of the camp, or in later times, Jerusalem, to prepare water for purification from sin.

The Cohenim were the leaders of Israel. Leaders have to be pure. The cow represents the Messiah Yeshua, who would be offered as a sacrifice. He provides living water, which flows from heaven like a wellspring, in order to cleanse the leadership of his earthly community. Also, none may approach the heavenly temple unless they are first made ritually clean by the messiah. There are so many more lessons to be gleaned from this whole thing, in regards to the hyssop, cedar wood and the scarlet yarn, but that would much to long for the purpose of this book. Just remember as you are reading all of these examples, compare them to the life and mission of Rabban Yeshua Ha Notzri (Master Yeshua of Nazareth) who I believe is the embodiment of all of these concepts. You have to have a firm knowledge of his life in order to make these connections

What about the serpent on the pole? This story is found in B'midbar 21. The people had accused G-d of bringing them out into the desert in order to torment them to death with bad food and thirst. These people began to curse the manna which the Ancient Holy One, blessed be his name, had been feeding them with. So in a sense, since the manna represents the messiah as the bread which came down from heaven, the people were rejecting G-d's plan of redemption, calling it a curse! G-d then sends an army of poison snakes and hundreds of people are bitten. Verses 7-9 ;

> Then the people came to Moshe and said, we have sinned, for we have spoken against ADONAI and against you. Pray to ADONAI to take away the serpents from us." Moshe prayed on behalf of the people. And ADONAI said to Moshe, "Make a fiery serpent and set it on a pole. And it shall be that everyone who is bitten, when he looks at it, shall live."So Moshe made a bronze serpent and put it on a pole. And it came to be if a serpent had bitten anyone, when he looked at the bronze serpent, he lived. [B'midbar (Numbers) 21: 7 – 9]

This seems to be just some strange episode, and some people write it off and move on. But the Ruach Ha Kodesh has carefully arranged the Torah and nothing is out of place. As I said before, the Ancient Holy One, blessed be He, set all of the events into motion as types, models, and symbols of messiah's life and mission. He used these stories and thousands more, to create, by the pen of men, his message to the world.

What is going on? People cursed the bread which came down from heaven and then judgment was decreed from above. The people cried out to G-d, who himself provided the plan for their salvation. However, they had to have faith. Faith in order to believe that what G-d said was true. G-d would not make any of them look at the bronze serpent. elevated upon a pole . This symbolized the manner in which mochiach was to die. Hung on a pole, cursed like a serpent because of the sins of his people. This is why Yeshua Ha Mochiach said;

> "As Moshe lifted up the serpent in the wilderness. So must the Son of Man be lifted up."

What became of this bronze serpent on the pole. Amazingly enough, it survived for centuries, down to the times of the Judean King, Hezekeyahu (Hezekiah). By this time the Jews who had betrayed Hashem and turned pagan, were worshiping this as an idol. It symbolized for them some entity called *Nehushtev*. The King had it broken up as part of his religious reform in the Kingdom of Yudah. Is not that our habit as humans? We take that which G-d had intended for good, and turn it into into a curse, twisting it into evil anti-Torah doctrines. King Hezekeyahu represents the messiah, who will put all of this to an end. He will brake up their Nehushtev!

I want to discuss the goats of **Yom Kippur**. How do these represent both the true messiah, and a false messiah? It should now be clear, that the sin offerings, the *Asham offerings* which are required, and the guilt offerings, are all intended by G-d to establish the concept of vicarious atonement. These were the shadow of what was to come. Messianic Rabbi John Popp said in a sermon at Beth Shalom Messianic Fellowship, Coeur d' Alene, Idaho on August 28th, 2010.

> "These things are a shadow. If you take away
> the Messiah, there is no shadow."

What Rabbi Popp was trying to explain was, that without the Messiah, none of this makes any sense. There would be no reason for all of these things.

Yom Kippur. The Day of Atonement. It is the most sacred day that the Bible commands us to observe. It is not a feast. It is a fast. B'midbar (Numbers) 29:7;

> And on the tenth day of this seventh month you are to have a Holy Convocation. And you shall afflict your beings, you do no work.

This verse established Yom Kippur as a fast, and as a High Sabbath. A Shabbat Gadol or a *Shabbatan*. It is a day when one sets aside all worldliness. It is a day of fasting and prayer, crying out to Almighty G-d for forgiveness of all your sins. The Day of Atonement for sins. Vayikra (Leviticus) 16: 30-31;

For on that day the priest shall make atonement for you, to cleanse you, that you may be clean from all your sins before ADONAI. It is a sabbath of solemn rest for you, and you shall afflict your souls. It is a statute forever.

Vayikra 23:26-28;

> And ADONAI spoke to Moshe saying: "Also the tenth day of this seventh month shall be the Day of Atonement. It shall be a holy convocation for you; you shall afflict your souls, and offer an offering made by fire to ADONAI. And you shall do no work on that same day, for it is the Day of Atonement to make atonement for you before ADONAI your G-d.

The Torah lists a precise sequence of ceremonies and sacrifices that the priests of Israel were instructed by the LORD to bring. This can be found in Vayikra chapter 16. Yom Kippur has very much to do with the messiah, because the whole concept of Yom Kippur is vicarious atonement. During the middle ages in Eastern Europe, long after the destruction of the Biet Ha Mikdash (Temple), a curious ritual developed amongst the Jews called, Kapparot. This word literally means, *"expiations"* with the idea of covering over or atoning. This comes from the word, Kippur, and from this we get the term, *Kippah*, which is the head covering that we wear to identify ourselves as Jews, and also in worship. So the ritual of Kapparot began in the ninth century by some Jewish groups who felt the need for a blood sacrifice, but could not comply with the instructions recorded in the Torah, due to the fact that the Biet Ha Mikdash was no longer in existence. The Torah, once given, had forbidden the building of high places and altars, in the way that Avraham had done. It is written;

> "Guard yourself that you do not offer your burnt offerings in every place that you see, except in the place which ADONAI chooses, in

one of your tribes. There you are to offer your burnt offerings, and there you are to do all that I command you." [D'varim, chapter 12:13-14]

Given this reality, on the day before Yom Kippur, they would take a chicken and swing it three times over their head while reciting the following prayer;

"This is my substitute, my vicarious offering, my atonement. This Rooster (for women it was a hen) shall meet death, but I shall find a long and pleasant life of peace."(Jewish Jewels, Yom Kippur Issue 2010

I will speak of more details about Yom Kippur ritual later, but now I must get to the main point that I had in bringing up Yom Kippur in the first place. The two sacrificial goats. These are both a symbol of; a true messiah and a false messiah, and they also symbolize a prophecy concerning Mochiach ben Yosef, the suffering messiah.. In ancient Judaism, the Rabbis developed this concept, in order to try and explain simultaneous prophecies, which speak of the messiah as a both a conquering King, and a suffering servant. They decided that there would be two messiahs, each coming once. However, in Messianic Judaism, *Mochiach ben Yosef*, and *Mochiach ben Dovid*, are one and the same. We have one messiah, coming twice, and the one messiah is Mochiach ben Elohim. The issue is; not did a man become G-d. That is impossible and is blasphemy. The issue is, G-d becoming a man in the body of the Messiah Yeshua. Cannot G-d, being almighty, do anything? Of course he can. Just because He doesn't fit the box that traditional Judaism attempts to put G-d in, does not make it less so.

Azazel is the Hebrew word which means, *scapegoat*. (there is a dark fallen angel by this name as well.) The root of this word includes the concept of removal. Part of the duties of the Cohen Gadol (High Priest) on Yom Kippur involved two male goats. Lots, or dice, were cast to determine which one of the goats would be, "for ADONAI, and which one would become the scapegoat, or *Azazel*. The Cohen Gadol would tie a piece of crimson-dyed wool between the horns of the scapegoat, and would tie a similar piece of wool around the neck of the goat which was to be sacrificed. This was based on the scripture verse in Yeshayahu 1:18

"Come now, and let us reason together," says ADONAI."Though your sins are like scarlet, they shall be as white as snow; though they are red like crimson, they shall be as wool."

The Cohen Gadol would then sacrifice the goat for the LORD, gather the blood into a basin, and enter into the Holy of Holies. Once inside he would sprinkle the blood on the top of the Ark of the Covenant, between the Keruvim. This part of the Ark is known as the Mercy Seat. This is where G-d spoke to Moshe. This blood was the atonement for the sins of Israel. Next, the Cohen Gadol would lay his hands on the head of the scapegoat, and confess over him all of the sins, iniquities, and transgressions of the people of Israel. It was then that the Azazel (scapegoat) was handed over to a specially dedicated Cohen (Priest) who would lead it off into the wilderness to a cliff. When the Azazel arrived at the cliff, the Cohen removed the crimson wool from its horns and divided it in half. One piece was tied onto the horns once more, and the remaining half to a part of the cliff. The Azazel Goat was then pushed backwards off of the cliff, bearing the sins of the people as it plunged to its death

Our Jewish traditions tell us that the piece of crimson wool turned white each year. This miracle was G-d's way of letting us know that He had accepted the sacrifices, and that atonement had been made for the sins of the people. It is stated in the Mishna that forty years before the destruction of the Holy Temple in 70 C.E., the crimson wool stopped turning white. This has been attributed by the Rabbis as being the result of Israeli Apostasy. However, we know from history, that this coincides with the death and the resurrection of Rabban Yeshua Ha Mochiach, who was the great atoning sacrifice.

How does Yom Kippur relate to the messiah? Even though the death of Rabban Yeshua did not occur on Yom Kippur, the events of that day during Passover, fulfill the model of the Goats of Yom Kippur. Did you know that there were two Yeshua's that day? Both of these had been put on trial and convicted. There was Yeshua of Nazareth, the suffering messiah, or *Mochiach ben Yosef*, and then there was *Yeshua bar Abba*. (Barrabas) This Yeshua bar Abba was a commander in the Jewish underground \ anti-Roman resistance movement known as the Zealots. Yeshua bar Abba was a military leader and a man who offered Israel a military solution to the Roman occupation. Both of the messiahs that day were being examined. The Mochiach ben Yosef was dragged away and murdered, while Yeshua bar Abba was released, and fled into the wilderness! He was later killed by the Romans. Yeshua Ha Mochiach was sacrificed to atone for the sins of mankind, and Yeshua bar Abba was the scapegoat. The people that day, were given a choice. Instead of the true messiah, they chose a false messiah. This is no coincidence.

To close out our discussion on the subject of Yom Kippur, I will talk about more customs and traditions, past and present, and introduce you to some terminology. The following is adapted from Jewish Jewels, Yom Kippur Issue, 2010., with my own insights added in. Jewish Jewels is a Florida based Messianic Jewish Ministry, founded by Neil and Jamie Lash.

Avodah;
The Avodah is a very significant part of the liturgy for the traditional Yom Kippur service. During the Avodah the multifaceted duties of the Cohen Gadol during Temple times on Yom Kippur are recounted. These are found in Vayikra (Leviticus) chapter 16. Shabbatan during Temple times centered around the High Priest (Cohen Gadol). This was an extremely demanding series of duties. He had to prepare himself for seven days, and was required to stay up all night, on the day before the fast. He ate very little and had to memorize every procedure, in order to assure that it was properly carried out. He went into Mikveh (Baptism) for

ritual purification. Everything had to be done exactly as commanded in the Torah, lest the Cohen Gadol be struck down by the LORD. Only he could enter the Holy of Holies, and then only once a year on Yom Kippur. There was a very real fear, awe, and respect for the LORD connected with Yom Kippur.

Chet*(guttural, cHet)*

This means, sin. If there were no sin, then there would not be a need for either Yom Kippur or the Mochiach ben Yosef. However, modern Rabbinic Judaism has strayed away from the biblical and Torah concept of sin. Modern mainstream forms of Judaism do not believe in original sin, but believe that we are all born with a pure soul, which can be kept clean by one's own determination. The yetzer ra, or evil inclination can be conquered by ones own effort and works. In spite of all the teaching of the past Rabbis, modern Judaism has rejected the concept of vicarious atonement, in order to escape or to get around Mochiach ben Yosef, whom they have rejected. Some Jews today, in spite of the Torah, even have rejected the whole concept of sin! I find this amazing in the wake of Nazism and Islamo-fascism. However this is not true of all Jews, especially Messianic Jews. We know that we have fallen short. This is the meaning of chet. And that is why you will find us in our Synagogues every year, reciting the Al Chet prayer. This long prayer, a lengthy confession of our sins, is based upon the confession of Nehemyah (Nehemiah) In Nehemyah 1:6;

> "Please let Your ear be attentive, and Your eyes open, that You may hear the prayer of your servant which I pray before you now, day and night, for the children of Israel Your servants, and confess the sins of the children of Israel which we have sinned against you.

The lesson from all of this is that chet can only be removed from us in the way that G-d has ordained and it is the vanity of man to assume otherwise.

Dahm*;*

This is the Hebrew word for blood. The sacrificial system laid out by the Torah involves a large amount of blood. It was ugly indeed. G-d is teaching a hard lesson here. Even as the blood and death involved in the sacrifices are ugly, even so sin is sick and ugly. During Temple times the entire Kidron Valley east of Jerusalem smelled of the stench of blood, which was continually being washed down out of the Temple precincts. Another reason for all of this blood is that it is a representation of life. Sin brought death. Only life can restore life. As I have said before, covenants were sealed in blood. Also, we are forbidden to eat blood. The shedding of blood is G-d's way of vicarious atonement, and makes us right with him. Vayikra 17:11;

> "For the life of the flesh is in the blood, and I have given it to you upon the altar to make atonement for your souls; For it is the blood that makes atonement for the soul."

Soon the Temple will be rebuilt, and those Jews who have been rejecting vicarious atonement are going to be in for a rude awakening. Make a visit to the Temple Institute in Jerusalem, or go to their website. And when Rabban Yeshua returns, this time as Messiah son of David, he will rule the world from the great Temple, which was shown to the Prophet Yehezqel (Ezekiel) and there will be sacrifices offered up there also.

Tefillah, Teshuvah, Tzedakah;

Prayer, Repentance, and Charity. In Rabbinic Judaism, these three practices have replaced the blood of atonement. This happened as a result of the destruction of the Beit Ha Mikdash (Temple) and the scattering of the Priesthood. Prayer has become the substitute for sacrifices, since it was spoken by the Prophet Hoshea, in 14:2

"Let us render for bullocks, the offering of our lips."

A *very large body of prayers are recited for forgiveness, Selichot, are recited during the entire season of the High Holy Days. Charity (Tzedakah) has become a second substitute. For the Rabbis wrote in the Talmud, in tractate Bava Batra 10a

"Charity delivers from death."

Now I think that the most important substitute for vicarious atonement is Teshuvah (Repentance) It is pointed out by modern Rabbinic Judaism, that the LORD G-d spoke through his Prophet Hoshea

> "I have no pleasure in the death of the wicked, but that the wicked turn from his way and live"

Teshuvah means," to turn." So we have the concept here of a complete turning around. Going the other way, and then asking for forgiveness. Repentance must precede redemption, but it is only a part of the way that G-d established for atonement.

Tzohm

Fasting is a major part of Yom Kippur, and this is what is meant by the term, "afflict your soul", in Vayikra 16 and 23. This is based on the interpretation given by the prophet Yeshayahu (Isaiah),58:3, about the humbling of the soul through fasting. Fasting on Yom Kippur is from sunset to sunset. All 24hours.

Vidui

Vidui(Vih-doo-EE)is the Hebrew word which means,"confession" Verbal confession is in inseparable from repentance. Confession is usually done corporately by the entire congregation. In Jewish tradition, as each sin is mentioned, the worshipers lightly strike the left sides of their chest. This implies that the heart is responsible for sin. And why do we do this as a body of believers, as well as personal prayers of confession to G-d? Because we take upon ourselves the guilt that results from us being a part of a sinful world. And this is what the Messiah was prophesied to do, and we model this during Yom Kippur by corporately confessing our sins.

Yamim Noriam

Yom is the Hebrew word for, "day." The plural is yamim. "Days." Nora is the word which means, awesome. So This term means, "Awesome Days", or more commonly, "Days of Awe." These are the days which fall between the Feast of Trumpets, "Yom Teruah" and Yom Kippur. The Rabbis teach that G-d judges on Yom Teruah, whether or not a person's name will be inscribed into the book of life. And then for the next ten days, we have the opportunity to reflect upon our lives, repent of sin, and to then reconcile with our fellow man. The Rabbis teach that on Yom Kippur, our fate is sealed, based upon our change of heart, or lack thereof. For this reason, Yom Kippur is also known as The Day of Judgment.

Zevachim

because G-d established his first Covenants with the fathers of all men, Adam and then Noach.

The sacrifices of animals during the times of the Mishkan and the Temple, were a a model of vicarious atonement. What we have going on here is an, exchange of life, principle. The lives of these innocent animals substituted for the life of a penitent sinner. There is a Divinely-appointed way to G-d which leads to an everlasting walk with the Holy One, blessed be his name. The sinner's way unto the Holy G-d of Avraham, Yitzaak, and Ya'ocov is by; a substitutionary sacrifice offered through Divinely-appointed High Priestly Mediation. This results in righteousness being imparted by Hashem (G-d) to the sinner, because of the death of the sinless sacrifice in place of the sinner. We as Messianic Jews, share this Concept of Messiah with the Christians, that it was Yeshua ha Notzri who fulfilled all of these by his own vicarious atonement. But not just for the lost sheep of Israel, but for the entire world. This

This will conclude our section on *Yom Kippur*, and I hope this sheds plenty of light on how, G-d has brought about redemption for this sin-sick world in which we live, by offering up himself as the sacrificed Goat of Yom Kippur, in the form of Yeshua ha Mochiach. But sadly, too few answer his call. Be set free. Be cleansed. Receive the Messiah by faith. Begin a new life.

I will end this section with a curious quote from *Zohar IV, 2:38b*.

> When the judgments of the Blessed Holy One seek to scrutinize the world, eying it—as it is written: The eyes of YHVH range over the whole earth (Zakarya 4:10)--and if they find wicked ones in

> the generation, then the righteous one in the generation is seized for their sins As for the wicked, the Blessed Holy One delays his anger, waiting for them to repent; and if not, no one is found to plead mercy for them, as it is written: a righteous one perishes in his righteousness—because he is righteous, he is removed from the world. (Zohar IV, Parasha Bo, 2:38b; Pritzker addition)

Even the writings of the Jewish Mystics speak of this theme. This time, not of an animal sacrifice, but a a righteous man making atonement for mankind This is the messiah of which the *Zohar* speaks.

How is the Messiah the Son of G-d? G-d is so vast and you cannot comprehend him. But there are some aspects which he has allowed us to be able to understand, even if in a limited way. The unknowable part we refer to as *Ein Sof*, or *Ke'ter*. From this you get, *Binah* (understanding) balance by *Hokhmah* (Wisdom). From these flow *Din* (Judgment) which is balanced by *Hesed* (Love). This gives rise to *Tif'eret* in the center, which is *messiah*. And from this come *Hod* (Splendor and Prophecy) which is balanced by *Netsah* (Endurance) From all of the above aspects of G-d, flows *Yesod* (Foundation) and within the foundation is *Ha Zaddek*, (Righteous One) which is the *physically manifested Messiah*. And from him flows *Malkut* (Kingdom) and *Shekhinah* (Glory) What does the Psalmist have to say about it? In the book of Tehillim (Psalms), number 2 ;

> Why do the gentiles rage, and the people meditate emptiness? The Kings of the earth take their stand, and the rulers take counsel together, against the Holy One and his Messiah and say, "Let us tear apart Their bonds, and throw away their ropes from us." He who is sitting in the heavens laughs, ADONAI mocks at them. Then He speaks to them in his wrath, and troubles them in his rage saying, "But I have set my King in Zion, My Holy Mountain." "I inscribe for a law:ADONAI has said to me, 'You are My Son. Today I have begotten you. Ask of Me, and I make the gentiles Your inheritance. And the ends of the earth Your possession. Break them with a rod of iron. Dash them to pieces like a potter's vessel.'

> "And now be wise, O Kings; Be instructed, you rulers of the earth. Serve ADONAI with fear, and rejoice with trembling. Kiss the Son, lest he be enraged, and you perish in the way. For soon His wrath is to be kindled. Blessed are those taking refuge in him.

Delving into this passage of scripture, we find it to be an amazingly esoteric and mystical teaching. In short order it declares that the messiah is the *Son of G-d*. That he was begotten by G-d and that he is part of G-d himself. Only begotten in ways unfathomable by man or even angels. This concept of messiah, put forth directly by the Holy Scriptures, declares not only that the messiah is, Ben Elohim, but that the warring nations of this entire world will be brought under the rule of the messiah. Modern mainstream Rabbis try to say that this refers to King David. However even Rashi, the French Rabbi from the era of the first crusade wrote how the Rabbis expounded it as speaking about King Messiah. This should tell you something, in light of the fact that Rashi is the one who went through the Tanakh and reinterpreted the prophecies of a suffering messiah to be referring to the people of Israel. A teaching that no Rabbi before his day expounded. Rashi did this, in response to Catholic persecution of the Jewish people.

This psalm also declares that those who put their trust in the messiah, will be given grace and a new life. The nature of the messiah here as the Divine Son is clearly established. Even King Shlomo (Solomon) wrote about the *Divine Son*

> Who has gone up to the heavens and come down? Who has gathered the wind in his fists? Who has bound the waters in his garment? Who has established the ends of the earth? What is his name? And what is his Son's name, if you know it? Every Word of ELOAH is tried. He is a shield to those taking refuge in him..
> [Mishle (Proverbs) 30: 4-5]

Shlomo is making statements in the form of questions. He speaks of how G-d is the one who is in control of all natural forces, and that he is the one who has created the earth. Then he declares that G-d has a **Divine Son**. In verse five he combines both Father and Son as ELOAH. One G-d, not using the dual form of Elohim. And then Shlomo declares that He, G-d, will shield all of those who put their trust in him. Mochiach Ben Elohim.

Concerning the name of the Divine Son, it had not yet been revealed, but the implication is clear. That it is YHVH, the sacred name of G-d. The fact that in the days of Shlomo, the Son's name had not yet been revealed, is not unusual in the Bible. Back in the beginning, even the name of G-d was not revealed. Not even to Adam, Noach, or Avraham. It was only revealed much later, when the Torah was given to Moshe on Mount Sinai

As I said, Man cannot become G-d! That is blasphemy. But can G-d become a man? Of course he can if he is G-d. Remember that he is ultimately Ke'ter, Ein Sof, the Unknowable Creator, who had to withdraw part of his light; part of himself; in order to create a space in which creation could dwell. No man can see the *Ein Sof* and live. He can see the mochiach aspect and live, but never the *Ein Sof*. Muslims and Rabbinic Jews who deny this, are putting G-d into a box in which He will not fit in order to further their own agendas. The Prophet Yeshayahu brought out this concept of messiah, when he wrote in his book, in chapter 9:6-7;

> For a child shall be born unto us, a Son shall be given unto us, and the government is on His shoulder. And his name is called Wonderful, Counselor, Mighty G-d, Everlasting Father, Prince of Peace. Of the increase of his Government there will be no end, upon the throne of Dovid and over his Kingdom, to establish it with justice and righteousness from now on, even forever. The zeal of the LORD of hosts does this.

This is a, G-d become man teaching. The Prophet proclaimed that the messiah would be born unto, *"us,"* the people of Israel, the Jews. The government was to be put on his shoulder. But then it goes into something which a mere man is not. It gives him the aspects of G-d.

It even refers to the messiah as Almighty G-d. It says that He will rule from the throne of *King David.* This means that this messiah must come from the family of King David, and yet still be G-d! This is so amazing!

Now this brings us to the next covenant on our step pyramid. The **Davidic Covenant**. Because Melech Dovid (King David) is from the House of Yudah. I will go back into the blessings which were given, first to Yudah by his father Ya'ocov, and then to the Tribe of Yudah by Moshe Rabbaneui.(Moses Our Teacher) The first blessing is found at the end of B'reshite in chapter 49:9-12;

> Yudah is a lion's cub; from the prey you have gone up my son! He bowed down, he crouched like a lion. And like a lion, who does rouse him? The scepter shall not turn aside from Yudah, nor a lawgiver from between his feet, until Shiloh comes, and to Him is the obedience of peoples. Binding his donkey to the vine, and his donkey's colt to the choice vine, he washed his garments in wine, and his robes in the blood of grapes. His eyes are darker than wine, and his teeth whiter than milk.

This is a curious blessing. Immediately we see references to a young lion. This is where the term, *"Lion of Yudah,"* comes from. A lion is a symbol of royalty and in case there is any doubt, the very next verse speaks of a scepter. We all know that Kings, sitting on their thrones, wield a scepter as the symbol of their power. Next it speaks of a *lawgiver*. So in the first half of this scripture we learn that Yudah's decedent will be a warrior king. This is Melech Dovid (King David) The lawgiver would seem to refer to Shlomo, and others of the tribe of Yudah which have been righteous expounders of Torah. Then it says, *"until Shiloh comes."* This word means, *"To Whom It Belongs."* This is a direct prophecy of the messiah, but does not reveal his name. It declares that all people will be in service to him. The next half reveals that the messiah has a donkey, and a donkey colt. This sounds just like something fulfilled by Rabban Yeshua doesn't it? Next he is *washed in wine*. Both he and his robes. By now you know that wine is a covental symbol of blood. A meal shared with bread, salt, and wine, were another way that agreements are ratified in the middle east. We find Avraham doing this with Melchi Tzaddeck, who was a Priest-King at Salem. (Salem was later renamed Jebus, and then Jerusalem.)

Lastly, *'his eyes are darker than wine and his teeth whiter than milk."* Eyes are a window into the soul, and wine represents blood. The blood atones for the sins of the soul. His teeth are white and pure. Everything that proceeds from the mouth of the messiah is white and pure. Foul teeth give rise to foul breath. The breath represents the Holy Spirit, and the messiah's spirit is holy, and without a foul stench. The messiah's teeth are white as milk, because his body is perfect and without blemish. This is the passage of Torah, whereby we know that G-d has chosen Yudah ben Ya'ocov, to be the head of the family which would bring forth, not just the Kings of Israel, but to the messiah himself. G-d chose to incarnate himself into mankind, his own creation, through this particular Jewish family. What an honor indeed.

The next thing is the blessing by Moshe Rabbaneui to the Tribe of Yudah.

> And this of Yudah, and he said, "Hear, ADONAI, the voice of Yudah, and bring him to his people. His hands shall fight for him, and You be a help against his enemies.[D'varim chapter 33: 7]

Moshe is praying for the people of Yudah. He is asking G-d to hear their voice. *Voice?* Why does it not say, *Voices?* It is because it speaks here not of many voices, as of a multitude, but a single voice as of a man. For it says, *'bring him to his people."* Bring who? Bring King Messiah. "His hands shall fight for him." His hands, the messiah's hands shall fight for, *'him"* Who is *'him?"* It is also the messiah. King Messiah will fight for Yudah, whose enemies are His enemies. Next, *"and You be a help against his enemies."* The *"You,"* is the Blessed Holy One, and Moshe prays that Hashem will fight with the messiah against his enemies. *"His enemies,"* is also understood to be the enemies of the Jewish people, since the passage is also referring to the Jewish people. More specifically it refers, to the tribe of Yudah.

Davidic Covenant

So now that we have found the origins of the Royal Blessing, we go to the Davidic Covenant itself. 2nd Shemu'el (Samuel) 7:4-17. Here King Dovid is feeling that since he was dwelling in a palace, that G-d should have a temple. But the young King, while well intentioned, was not realizing that the LORD is much greater than he could perceive. He does not dwell in earthly temples. These types of shrines are for our sake, so that we may have a worship center. Not that Hashem needs a roof or a gate. But King Dovid's heart was in the right place, and Hashem honored him for it. The LORD even said himself that Dovid was, *"A man after G-d's own heart."*

> And it came to be that night that the word of ADONAI came to Nathan, saying Go and say to my servant Dovid,'Thus says ADONAI, "Would you build a house for me to dwell in? For I have not dwelt in a house since the time I brought the children of Israel up from Egypt, even to this day,but have moved about in a tent and in a Dwelling Place."Wherever I have walked with all the children of Israel, have I ever spoken a word to anyone from the tribes of Israel, whom I commanded to shepherd my people Israel saying, 'Why have you not built me a house of cedar?' ""And now say to my servant Dovid, ' Thus says ADONAI of hosts, "I took you from the pasture, from following the flock, to be ruler over My people, over Israel."And I have been with you wherever you have gone, and have cut off all of your enemies from before you, and have made you a great name, like the name of the great ones who are on the earth. "And I shall appoint a place for my people Israel, and shall plant them, and they shall dwell in a place of their own and no longer be afraid, neither shall the children of wickedness oppress them again, as at the first,even from the day I appointed rulers over my people Israel, and have caused you to rest from all of your enemies. And ADONAI has declared to you

that He would make you a house. "When your days are filled and you rest with your fathers, I shall raise up your seed after you, who comes from your inward parts, and shall establish his reign "He does build a house for My Name, and I shall establish the throne of his reign forever" I am to be his father, and he is be My son. If he does perversely, I shall reprove him with the rod of men and with the blows of the sons of men. "But my kindness does not turn aside from him, as I turned aside from Sha'ul, whom I removed from before you. "And your house and your reign are to be steadfast forever before you—your throne established forever."

'"According to all these words and according to all this vision, so Nathan spoke to Dovid.

The context of this was that the King wanted to build a temple. But G-d explained to Dovid, that he would build Dovid a house. Not a palace. Dovid already had one of those. The house of which Hashem is speaking is a *royal dynasty*. Through this dynasty, the promises made to Yudah would all come to pass, and that it would be an everlasting Kingdom. This promise is only obtainable for Melech Dovid, if one of his descendents is immortal.

There are numerous passages in the prophets which speak to the Davidic Covenant. But I will keep this short and limit it to two in particular, which stands out to me.

And a Rod shall come forth from the stump of Yishai, and a sprout from his roots shall bear fruit. [Yeshayahu (Isaiah) 11:1]

Yishai (Jesse) is the father of King Dovid. Why does it say, *"from the stump of Yishai?"* Because the royal house was to be *cut off*. Chopped down. But G-d would still honor the pledge made to Dovid, that his royal line would be established forever for he said, *"a sprout from his roots shall bear fruit"*. This sprout is King Messiah, who must be immortal. Why immortal? Because the LORD said unto Dovid, *"And your house and your reign (Kingdom) are to be steadfast forever."* It is also written, (Yeshayahu 11:1)

> And in that day there shall be a root of Yishai, standing as a banner to the people. Unto him the gentiles shall seek, and his resting place shall be glorious.

Again the prophet refers to Yishai as a tree. Why does it say, *"standing as a banner,"*? Because King Messiah shall arise and lead his people to victory. The nations of the world will come to know the G-d of heaven through Rabbi King Messiah. Why does it say, *"his resting place shall be glorious"*? Because Shekinah is the the true glory of the kingdom, and the place of his rest is, Jerusalem. In his Holy Temple, Rabbi King Messiah is G-d's Shekinah on earth.

There are so many, many passages in the book of Yeshayahu about the messiah, many in the Psalms as well. Go forth and find them and in reading them, you will see the paradox. They put forth the two roles of the messiah, within the same breath. It is clear from all of this, that the things the messiah must do, are things of which no mere mortal can accomplish.

One Psalm in particular that is clearly a Prophecy about the Mochiach Ben Yosef is Psalm 22: 1-21;

> My G-d, my G-d, why have you forsaken me-far from the words of My groaning? Oh My G-d, I call by day, but you do not answer; And by night, but I find no rest, Yet You are holy, enthroned on the praises of Israel. Our fathers trusted in you, and were not ashamed. But I am a worm, and no man. A reproach of men and despised by the people. All those who see Me mock Me; They shoot out the lip, they shake the head saying, "He trusted in ADONAI, let him rescue Him; Let Him deliver Him, seeing He has delighted in Him!" For you are the one who took Me out of the womb; Causing Me to trust while on my mother's breasts. I was cast upon you from birth. From My mother's belly, You have been my G-d. Do not be far from Me, for distress is near; For there is none to help. Many bulls have surrounded me; Strong ones of Bashan have encircled Me. They have opened their mouths

> against Me, as a raging and roaring lion. I have been poured out like water, and all My bones have been spread apart; My heart has become like wax; It has melted in the midst of my inward parts. My strength is dried like a potsherd, and my tongue is cleaving to my jaws; And to the dust of death you are appointing me. For dogs have surrounded me; A crowd of evil ones have encircled Me, piercing my hands and my feet. I count all my bones. They look, they stare at me. They divide my garments among them, and for my raiment they cast lots. But You oh ADONAI, do not be far off; Oh my strength,hasten to help me! Deliver my life from the sword, My only life from the power of the dog. Save me from the mouth of the lion, and from the horns of wild beasts! You have answered me. I make known Your Name to my brothers; in the midst of the assembly I praise You.

There is a whole lot of explicit details in this. Here is a summary of it all. The messiah is forsaken by G-d. Then he is mocked, tormented and ridiculed by the people. Gamblers divide up his clothing via a game of dice. His agony is so severe that his bones become disjointed. His heart breaks with a mixture of blood and water. Then his hands and feet are pierced. How cruel and vicious! Yet this same messiah is also a conquering King! No mortal man can accomplish both. The messiah has to be an immortal. The ancient Rabbis in Midrash Yalkut referred this passage of scripture to, the messiah, the Son of Yosef.

Next we move on to the most famous passage of scripture. Yeshayahu (Isaiah) chapter 53. We will first read the chapter, interpret the chapter, and then discuss the debate that we have with Rabbinic Jews as to whom or what it refers.

> Who has believed our report? And to whom was the arm of ADONAI revealed? For He grew up before Him as a tender plant, and as a root out of dry ground. He has no form or splendor that we should look upon Him, nor appearance that we should desire Him—despised and rejected by men, a man of pains and knowing sickness. And as one for whom the face is hidden, being despised,

and we did not consider Him. Truly, He has born our sicknesses and carried our pains. Yet we reckoned Him stricken, smitten by G-d, and afflicted. But He was pierced for our transgressions, He was crushed for our iniquities. The chastisement for our peace was upon Him, and by his stripes we are healed. We all like sheep have gone astray, each one of us has turned to his own way. And ADONAI has laid upon him the iniquities of us all. He was oppressed and He was afflicted, but He did not open His mouth. He was led like a lamb to slaughter, and as a sheep before its shearers is silent, yet He did not open His mouth. He was taken from prison and from judgment. And as for His generation who considered that He shall be cut off from the land of the living? For the transgressions of My people He was stricken. And He was appointed a grave with the wicked, and with the rich at his death, because He had done no violence, nor was deceit in His mouth. But ADONAI was pleased to crush Him, He laid sickness on Him, that when He made Himself an offering for guilt, He would prolong His days, and the pleasure of ADONAI prosper in His hand. He would see the result of the suffering of His life and be satisfied. Through His knowledge My righteous Servant makes many righteous, and He bears their iniquities. Therefore I give Him a portion among the great, and He divides the spoil with the strong, because He poured out His life unto death, and He was counted with the transgressors, and He bore the sin of many, and made intercession for the transgressors.

We have here, a detailed account of the mission of Mochiach ben Yosef. The suffering servant messiah. This tells us the why, and the results. It tells of his death, and in a very unique and colorful way, it prophecies his resurrection.

Let's go into it bit by bit, one piece at a time. *"Who has believed our report?"* This because our people Israel will not believe the words of the witnesses concerning Rabbi King Messiah. *"To whom was the arm of ADONAI revealed?"* This is said because the strong will of the Blessed Holy One is revealed through Rabbi King Messiah.

"He grew up as a root out of dry ground" This because the soil of the hearts of the men of Israel were dry and did not have the living water of the Holy Spirit of G-d. Yet Rabbi King Messiah grew up in fear and respect of the Blessed Holy One, because G-d gave him the water of the the Holy Spirit, *"He has no form or splendor that we should look upon Him."* This is so, because the Rabbi King Messiah was not to be born in a royal palace, but in meek and humbleness, as befitting of his spirit. He would not be as the pompous Kings of men are. His splendor is to be given by the LORD G-d, blessed be His Name, and not of the fickleness of men. *"Nor appearance that we should desire Him."* Rabbi King Messiah does not dwell in Temples made by the hand of man, nor does he regard the wealth and looks of the arrogant rich, who lord over the working man. Rabbi King Messiah, here in this manifestation, shall have the look of a laborer, so that he may walk as one of them, but having the word of the Living G-d, uttering from his lips.

"Despised and rejected by men," Those of his generation will then hate and reject his words, because he came not in the manner which they desired. He came. *"meek and humble, riding upon a donkey,"* (Zakarya 8: 9) because Israel was found unworthy. *"Knowing sickness"* because he saw the many who were ill, and heals them, all who come to him. Those sent to him by the Blessed Holy One, Rabbi King Messiah will not send away. *"And as one from whom the face is hidden."* That generation will not see that he comes from heaven, and will turn from Rabbi King Messiah, and hide their faces. Some will hide their faces in shame! For they said they believed in Him, but when the time came for them to stand with Rabbi King Messiah, they shamefully hid their faces, and fled away. Let us not do likewise. *"Being despised,"* Those of his generation will hate what Rabbi King Messiah stands for. He stands for truth and justice, honor and Torah. Those corrupt men in that generation shall indeed despise Rabbi King Messiah, for

they see in him, that which they cannot be. *"We did not consider him"* Yes, we did not consider him. Even those who live in his own village do not consider Him, for it is said, *"A prophet has no honor in his own country."* (Besuras Hageulah of Lukas 4:24)

"Truly He has born our sickness and carried our pain" Rabbi King Messiah shall see the sickness of our souls, and by lifting of our pain, shall indeed cleanse our spirits. Yet also shall he heal those who come unto him, for it is said, *"The Sun of Righteousness shall arise, with healing in his wings."* (Malachi 4:2) *"Yet we reckoned him stricken."* This is said because, those of his generation, and many after, shall deem Rabbi King Messiah to be a sinner struck down, and his people shall say a false messiah has been purged. *"Smitten by G-d and afflicted.."* This is said by those who said he died by the hand of G-d for his blasphemy.

"But He was pierced for our transgressions." Rabbi King Messiah would not be impaled for anything He Himself had done, but only for those things which the wicked of this world have committed in the casting aside of His Torah. *"Pierced"* This is the manner in which Rabbi King Messiah must perish. *"He was crushed (bruised) for our iniquities."* Rabbi King Messiah must be a martyr because if not, then all men will perish in sin. *"Crushed (bruised)"* Because those who pierce Him do also bruise and crush his body and torment him unto death. *"The chastisement of our peace was upon Him."* Our souls would have no peace in the world to come, nor in this world now, if not for Rabbi King Messiah, who would except our chastisement. He who is lord has become, *"a ram caught in the bush by its horns."* (B'reshite 22:13) *"By his stripes we are healed."* Know by this, that Rabbi King Messiah is prophesied to be beaten with whips, which make upon him bloody stripes. Stripes from which flow blood which does make atonement for the sinners among men, for it says, *"we are healed."* Why, *"we"*? Because all who come are healed. Not many by the standard of the world that is now. But the *"we"* who are called according to his purpose. Even as were the seven thousand out of all Israel were called

by the Blessed Holy One in the days of Eliyahu the Prophet (1st Melakim{Kings}19:18

"We all, like sheep." Men are often like sheep. Wondering around looking at the grass in the pasture. Moving from clump to clump, never looking up, until they are lost and exposed to the wolves. Sheep are easily oppressed, as are people. This is why it is said, *"Went astray"*, each of us has turned to his own way." Why, *"his own way"*? Because men preferred to rule in hell, rather to serve in heaven. Indeed are proud and arrogant. For it is just as it was in the days of Nimrod when they said, *"make a name for ourselves."* (B'reshite 11:4) *"And ADONAI has laid upon Him the iniquities of us all."* The Blessed Holy One charges Rabbi King Messiah with the blood guilt of the sons and daughters of man, and has laid it onto Rabbi King Messiah, as if it were a burdensome pack of rocks.

"He was oppressed and afflicted." The sons of man have oppressed and punished the innocent, Rabbi King Messiah, just as they do to all who represent justice and peace. *"But He opened not His Mouth."* The Blessed Holy One sent Rabbi King Messiah to accomplish this task, therefore in order that it be so, He would give no credible defense. Nor would he, by opening his mouth, call forth legions of angels to smite those who would oppress Him. *"As a lamb "* because Rabbi King Messiah has become the passover lamb " This is also why it is said, *"He was led like a lamb to slaughter."* The Rabbi King Messiah would go willing for his people to death, and without protest. Silently allowing himself to be taken to the abyss of death. Therefore the Prophet has written, *"as a sheep before its shearers is silent, but He did not open His mouth"*. Why *"a sheep"*? Because Rabbi King Messiah must become the guilt offering, for it is written, *"He shall bring to ADONAI as his guilt offering, a ram, a perfect one."* (Vayikra {Leviticus}7:15 & 7:18)

"He was taken from Prison" Wicked men of the nations would cast Rabbi king Messiah into jail as if he were a criminal or a pillager, *"From judgment"* because petty men would pretend to be a judge over him who knows no sin, and they themselves are corrupt in their legal

systems, which set up laws against men. Oppressors, all of them! Then and now and in all nations!.

"As for His generation, who considered that He shall be cut off from the land of the living." This is written, because no one who would live, and walk with, and learn from Rabbi King Messiah would have the thought in their minds, that He must first be martyred, before He could be King. Why must He be a martyr? *"For the transgression of my people He was stricken." "He was appointed a grave with the wicked."* Being taken from prison, Rabbi King Messiah was to be killed. Those who planned his murder considered him a criminal and a rebel, and thus would say He must be cast into she'ol with those for whom it was deserved. *"And with the rich at His death"*. This is said in order that one whose wealth was here in Israel, would have compassion, and thus bury Rabbi King Messiah in the tomb of the wealthy. This because Rabbi King Messiah, being meek and humble, had no tomb of his own, whereby his family might lay their innocent Son.

"He had done no violence." Rabbi King Messiah was no rebel. He was to be innocent of the charges brought against him by the *Bet Din*(Court). *"Nor was deceit in His mouth."* He must be falsely accused of abrogating the Torah of the Ancient Holy One, blessed be his name. A crime of which, were He guilty, be the ultimate deceit. However Rabbi King Messiah is to come, giving a greater, more perfect interpretation of the Torah. Even so much so, that He will interpret the spaces between the letters. Those who witness against him at Bet Din are sons of purgery, But from the lips of Rabbi King Messiah, comes nothing deceitful.

"But ADONAI was pleased to crush (bruise) Him." Is G-d here happy to inflict pain? Heaven forbid, no! HASHEM laid on Rabbi King Messiah, the sicknesses of the sins of the people, in order that none of them perish. But this only by the free choice of Rabbi King Messiah Himself, after He had been asked by the Holy One, blessed be His Name, to take up this burden. For it is written, *"He made himself an offering for guilt."* And if Rabbi King Messiah would do this, then the Holy One, blessed be His Name, would see those many souls who

would be saved from Geh-hinnom. He would see them planted and grow. Messiah himself would be cast into the grave, and yet because of this, his saved ones would grow as many as a field of wheat. Therefore it is written, *"He would see a seed."* But yet, Rabbi King Messiah must not stay in the earth. He must rise again from the ashes of his own tomb, for the prophet writes, *"He would prolong His days."* Indeed, the Blessed Holy One, after these things, shall give unto Rabbi King Messiah His Kingdom and He shall do what pleases the Ancient Holy One, blessed be His Name, here in Israel and on Earth, as it is written, *"the pleasure of ADONAI prosper in His hand."*

"He would see the results of the suffering of His life, and be satisfied." He who was put to death, must rise up from she'ol, and seeing the good which came from his suffering, would thus be pleased with the success. Indeed, all who now then come to the Risen One, whom the Blessed Holy Ones declares, *"My Righteous Servant,"* shall see their holy reward. The holy reward of being made by the **Risen One**, a righteous and an eternally living being. This because it is written, *"Through His knowledge My Righteous Servant makes many righteous, and bears their iniquities."* Why does it say,*"His Knowledge,"* ? Because the **Risen One** has knowledge of them. He is, as it were, a shepherd, who knows his sheep. Also this is written, so that we may know that men are saved by their knowledge of the **Risen One**. Not just of mind, but in heart, and declaration.

"Therefore I have given Him a portion among the great and he divides the spoil with the strong." The Blessed Holy One now makes the **Risen One who is** Rabbi King Messiah, a great conquering warrior King. For it is also said, *"He treads the winepress of the fierceness and wrath of Almighty G-d!"* (Hisgalus 19:15) Why does the Blessed Holy One do this for the **Risen One?** Because it is written *"He poured out His being unto death,"* and because it was the free choice of the Risen One to be as one of those of which He comes to save. For this reason it is written, *"He was counted with the transgressors and He bore the sin of many."* Why, *"the many"*? Because all men stand condemned of their

sins, and they are not just a few but, *"Many"*. *"And made intercession for the transgressors"* The Risen One comes, like a High Priest, to the Blessed Ein Sof, before whom a man cannot stand and live, and shows that the transgressing sinners of the sons and daughters of man, who belong to Rabbi King Messiah, the Risen One, blessed be His Name, are reconciled unto life everlasting. Amen.

And what says the *Zohar* concerning this? (Zohar, Pritzker addition by Daniel Matt)

> There is in the garden of Eden a palace called the Palace of the sons of sickness; this place the Messiah then enters, and summons every sickness, every pain, and every chastisement of Israel; they all come and rest upon him. And were it not that he had thus lighted them off Israel and taken them upon himself, there had been no man able to bear Israel's chastisement for transgression of the law: and this is that which is written, "Surely our sickness he had carried."

The *Zohar* refers to Rabbi King Messiah himself, and shows that Israel as a people are thus distinct from the messiah, spoken of by Yeshayahu the Prophet. And so the mystics of Israel recognized that Rabbi King Messiah takes upon himself the suffering for the sins of Israel. He is the substitute.

And finally we turn to the dispute. The ancient books of the *Targums* all referred to this passage as speaking of the messiah. Modern Talmudic Jewish Rabbis declare that this speaks, not of the messiah, but of the nation of Israel and the Jewish people. However, before the times of the Crusades, this was not so. The *Talmud Bavli*, assembled in Iraq during the 5th Century C.E. Always teaches that the 53rd chapter of Yeshayahu refers to the messiah. The quotes are drawn from, Everyman's Talmud by Abraham Cohen.

> The Messiah—what is his name?.....those of the house of Rabbi Yudah the Saint say, The sick one, as it is said, "Surely he had borne our sicknesses. (Sanhedrin 98b)

In Midrash Thanhumi there is this;

> Rabbi Nahman says, the word, "man" in the passage refers to the Messiah Son of David, as it is written, "Behold the man whose name is Zemah" there Yonatan interprets, Behold the man is Messiah; as it is said, "a man of pains and known to sickness."

Midrash Cohen

> Eliyahu (Elijah) says to Messiah, "Bear the suffering and punishment of thy Lord, which he chastises thee for the sins of Israel, as it is written, "He is pressed for our rebellion-crushed for our iniquities" until the end come.

Rabbi Eliezar Kalir, writing in the 7th century C.E. Composed the Musaf Prayer for the Yom Kippur Mahsor (Siddur or Prayer Book) Here is part of it.

> Messiah our Righteousness is departed from us:horror hath seized us, and we have none to justify us. He hath borne the yoke of our iniquities, and our transgression, and was wounded because of our transgression. He beareth our sins on his shoulder, that he may find pardon for our iniquities. We shall be healed by his wound, at the time that the Eternal will create him as a new creature. Oh bring him up from the circle of the earth. Raise him up from the land of Seir, to assemble us on Mount Lebanon, a second time by the power of Yinon.

Much of this prayer is a quotation from Yeshayahu 53, and this shows us, that as late as the seventh century C.E. Major Jewish thinkers all held the view that this passage of scripture referred to Rabbi King Messiah.

So when the change, and why? During the era of the First Crusade, there arose a Jewish Scholar and Rabbi, by the name of Shlomo Yizchaki. He is called, **Rashi**, which is a combination of the letters of his title and those of his name. He taught in Lyon, France, and had been forced by the Roman Catholic Church, into a series of debates. The debates centered around whether or not Jesus, as the Christians call him, was the messiah. These debates centered around passages like the ones in Yeshayahu. However, the outcome of these detestable kangaroo courts were pretty much predetermined from the outset. The result was that the Christians burned any copies of the Talmud that they could get their hands on, especially in Paris. Pope Urban II preached the First Crusade, and the Knights of France and Germany assembled to march to Jerusalem in order to expel the Muslim usurpers from the Holy City. Muslims were the infidel, and had to be driven away, so that they could no more threaten the west with their infamous Jihads.

However, there was a major problem. Not only does Islam consider the Jews heretics, but the Christians of this period, also considered our people to be,*"Christ Killers"* and *infidels*. As the Catholic Knights marched east, they ravaged the Jewish communities along the route of march. In the Rhineland of Germany, the French Knights under Godfrey of Buillion engaged in the sport of, how many Jewish babies can one impale on a single sword!(Even in these days, some Christian Zealot woman, talking to me, declared that the Jewish Religion was useless and had passed away, and that the Jews were the Christ Killers! In the same breath she claims to be a follower and a lover of G-d!

With all this in mind, I can understand Rashi. The Christian Killers of his people, were doing it in the name of Jesus of Nazareth! The tormentors declared that everything Jewish was blasphemy!That the Jews must convert or die! Many chose death. Who would want to follow the messiah of those killer Knights and wicked Priests of the inquisition! So much for Chivalry!

But how would you answer the Christians, who could firmly show that indeed, these passages did refer to Jesus of Nazareth, as the Christians call him. He had to give them new meaning, lest the Jewish people convert to Gentile Christianity. So Rashi went through the entire Jewish canon of scriptures and, in his commentaries, declared that all of the passages referring to a suffering messiah, did not refer to the messiah, but to the Jewish people as a whole. In spite of the reaction against this over time by men such as Rabbi Naphtali ben Asher Altschuler(c. 1650), Herz Homburg in his work,Korem, in 1818, it has become the dominant theme in Rabbinic Jewish theology. But it is not the traditional view. Those closer in time to the original writings, and who had much less, or no contact with either Christian apologetics or Christian persecutors, interpreted all of these types of passages in the scriptures, as referring to Rabbi King Messiah.

In concluding this chapter, Messianic Jews believe that the nature of the messiah, is that he is the divine Son of G-d. That G-d, became a man in the form of Yeshua Ha Notzri. That he is the culmination of everything the prophets spoke of. That he is both Mochiach ben Yosef, and Mochiach ben Dovid, and at the same time, Mochiach ben Elohim. That he is the one who made atonement, and then having returned from death, shall then again return as the conquering King. This view is shared with Messianic Jews by the Christians. However, Messianic Jews maintain biblical and Jewish forms of culture and worship. Because we are persecuted for it from both sides. From Rabbinic Orthodox Judaism, whose adherents consider us to be, Minim, (heretics), and from Christians (most but not all) who consider us to be a cult. A cult because, Messianics refuse to bow to their anti-Torah doctrines and cling fiercely to being Jews. We will not put aside the writings of Judaism, and exchange them for alternatives. Judaism, Messianic or otherwise, is a warm rich, living, colorful religion. It is a way of life for those who truly put it into practice. From the Bible, we have inherited a beautiful culture. Why would we want to give it up. It is good to us. Good for us.

Jesus The Christ,

(Some Christian Concepts of Messiah.)

We now leave the forms of Judaism, and turn to some common Christian concepts of messiah. I will point out from the outset, that this short work cannot contain all of the divergent doctrines of every denomination which goes under the name, Christian.

The Jews and the Christians share the same biblical prophecies when it comes to the messiah. As we have already dealt with this at length, we will not have to go back over all that ground again. The Church even shares many of the concepts of messiah brought forth in the *Targums,* the *Talmud,* and the *Midrashim*. But the Church, for the most part, has rejected these writings when forming doctrine. I would expect them to, because these writings are not part of their religious tradition. They especially reject the Zohar, because to these groups, Kaballah and the Mystical tradition of scripture is something they fear. Some think it evil. I am not here to condemn them, for I have already given my defense of Judaism in the last chapter. I am here to write about their, concepts of messiah. It would be inaccurate to say that there is one single, Christianity. There are many. Some sects that exist in India and Africa are older than European Christianity, and hark back to the days of the Apostles. In brief, I will share this history.

During the first century of the common era, there was no such thing as the institutions today which are collectively called, Christianity. There was Judaism, and from it, came Messianic Judaism. This was the framework in which converts were first brought in. These people were known as, "**The Way,**" and. "**Nazarenes.**" In fact, the term, "Christian," was used in that era as a pejorative. A very negative term, because there were some in the Roman Empire, who brought upon them a blood libel accusation. Because of the words of the messiah concerning his body being bread and his blood being drink, a wicked story spread west that these **Jews of The Way**, were engaging in cannibalism. A similar charge was that the Matzah bread of Passover was made with the blood of children. During this time, all Jews of any stripe were subject to terrible slaughter and persecution by the Romans.

In 68 C.E., a rebellion started in Judea by our people against Roman tyranny. Messianic Jews remembered the prophecy, given by Yeshua the Messiah, concerning Jerusalem;

> And as He came near, He saw the city, and wept over it, saying, "If you only knew even today, the matters for your peace! But now they are hidden from your eyes. Because days shall come upon you when your enemies shall build a rampart around you, and surround you and press you on all sides, and dash you to the ground, and your children within you. And they shall not leave in you one stone upon another, because you did not know the time of your visitation."[Lukas 19: 41 – 44]

Because they recognized that words of Rabbi King Messiah were coming to fulfillment, Messianic Jews (this includes the former Gentiles, who were now proselytes and fully Jewish) fled Judea ahead of the Roman Armies, to the city of Pella, east of the River Jordan. This drew the disdain of the rest of the Jews who were struggling against the Empire. The Temple was destroyed, and all vestiges of Judean government were annihilated in a fiery, bloody holocaust. The Pious *Essenes* managed to safely hide away their great works of Torah and communal literature in caves above the Dead Sea, before the Romans butchered them at Qumran. A small group of *Zealots* and *Essenes*, escaped to the fortress of **Masada**, and continued guerrilla warfare against the Roman forces. General Titus had destroyed the city and the sanctuary, but the command was now given to General Flavius Silva. Silva marched to Masada, and besieged the freedom fighters, who were led by Zealot Commander, **Eleazar ben Ya'ir** .Masada is located high on a mesa, and Silva brought in the siege master, Rubius Gallus. Silva rounded up 2000 Jewish slaves,forcing them to build a massive ramp. Also a tower on wheels was constructed, equipped with a battering ram. In 73 C.E. when the tower was rolled up the ramp, and the walls breached, Eleazar and the Zealots, along with the last of the *Essenes*, committed suicide, rather than to be taken and crucified.

The rest of Judaism began to persecute *The Way*, and over the next forty to fifty years, forced our ancestors out of the synagogues. But leaders like Rav Sha'ul (Apostle Paul) , Rav Yochanan Ha Shliach (Apostle John the Revelator) and their Talmidim (Disciples) had early on, brought Messianic Jews (this includes their Gentile converts like Luke) together in *Home Synagogues*. This formed the basic foundation of a new divergent form of Judaism, while still retaining all Biblical customs. *The Way* was now, on one hand, driven out by their Jewish brethren, and at the same time, viciously persecuted by the Romans, by now led by Emperor Domitian. These persecution fell on all Jews, because none would burn incense to any Caesar, whether he claimed to be a god or not.

In 133, another rebellion started, led by Zealot Commander, *Shimon bar Kosiba*, also know as Bar Kochba which means, *"Son of a Star."* Rabbi Akiva had declared Kosiba to be the messiah, and he demanded loyalty from all Jews in the Empire. Not only was there fighting in Judea, but there were riots and insurrections in Jewish communities across the Empire,from Egypt and Cyrenacia in North Africa, to Italy and Asia Minor. Jews of *The Way* were willing at first, at least in Judea, to fight along side of Kosiba and the rest of Israel. However, when Rabbi Akiva declared Kosiba to be the messiah, our ancestors could not continue to support the war. The Way had, for a century, declared that Yeshua Ha Notzri was the Rabbi King Messiah. By this time, the books of the New Testament were in circulation and all of these works proclaimed Yeshua. How could they then follow a man, whom they knew to be a false prophet and false messiah? They must have recalled the words spoken by Yeshua Messiah saying;

I have come in my Father's name, and you don't accept me; if someone else comes in his own name, him you will accept.[Yochanan 5;43]

I believe this to be a prophecy about Bar Kosiba In this time period between the destruction of the temple and the end of Bar Kosiba's war, came the great schism between, The Way Judaism, and what became, Rabbinic Judaism.

The Romans levied an evil tax, *fiscus Judaica,* on all Jews whether they be Jews by birth, or by conversion. Whether they be Rabbinic Jews, or Jews of The Way. The Way had thousands of former Gentiles who desired to get out from under this tax. The result now was another schism, between those whose blood lineage was Israel, and those who were gentile by birth. Gentile leaders, known to us as the *Anti-Nicaean Church Fathers*, began to react against their Rabbinic Jewish brethren, Jews were denounced, and the Jews by birth, who believed in Rabbi King Messiah, (who the Romans were now calling Jesus), were given the choice of; giving up their heritage, or expulsion. Gentile converts far outnumbered native born Jews in *The Way,* making such a thing possible. Thus was the gradual birth of the institutions called, the **Christian Church**. The Way died out as a movement with its own synagogues, until 1967 C.E. But always, down through the ages, ADONAI preserved a remnant, who faced rejection by the Jews, and persecution by the Christians for non-conformity. Many perished in the flames of the inquisition along with Protestants, Huguenots, Ana-Baptists, Lutherans, and Weslyans. These along with others who would not conform to the dogma of either Roman Catholicism, Eastern Orthodox, Russian Orthodox, Serbian Orthodox, or Greek Catholicism.

I must point out, that the modern Evangelicals are not included in the list of tormentors. They support Israel, even if they disagree with the stand for the Torah by modern Messianic Jews.

In the era of the **Emperor Constantine**, big changes came to the Christian Churches. A doctrine which has since become known as, *replacement theology* developed. This doctrine teaches that the Jews have been rejected as cast aside for killing Christ. And that G-d has replaced the people of Israel with the Church. From this comes the epithet, *Christ Killers*, which has been used against me, and by anti-Semite bigots down to this present era.

The Emperor Constantine, after crushing all of his rivals in series of bloody civil wars, began to favor Christianity. This after a vision of a cross in the sun, and a voice which proclaimed to him; "In this sign, conquer." He ordered the Greek letters **XP**, abbreviation for, **Christos**, inscribed on the shields of his Legionaries. Constantine's forces smashed the Army of Maxentius at Milvian Bridge. Once in full power, he issued the famous, *"Edict of Toleration,"* which declared Christianity to be a legal religion in the Roman Empire. It would not become the official state religion until the days of the Emperor Theodosius. In book 16 of the Theodosian code, paganism was outlawed, in the years 429-435. It has been taught that Constantine converted soon after the vision. However, in spite of his taking control of the Gentile Church, he never accepted baptism until he lay sick on his deathbed. So his conversion was a slow process, and not the instantaneous or sudden event that is spoken of in Catholic tradition.

Constantine I, has been given the title, *Constantine the Great*. He took charge over all the Bishops throughout the Empire. It was at this time, that a key concept of messiah developed. This was that Jesus Christ would not come back as a King in the echatological future, but that his Kingdom was purely spiritual. That all messianic prophecies had either been fulfilled in the past or had a purely spiritual meaning. You must remember, that Constantine believed himself to be, King of Kings. He, being Emperor, also held the title of, *"Pontiffus Maximus,"* or *"Supreme Pontiff."* This title meant that the Emperor was the supreme religious leader of the Empire. This is a title which is now held by the Pope of Rome. It was under this title and law, that the Emperors of the past like Nero, Domitian, Decius, Marcus Aurelius, Commodus, and Diocletian, were able declare which religions were legal and which of those were not.

When Christianity first began to be identified as a separate religion from Judaism, it was persecuted. This was because it was not a legally

Concepts of Messiah

recognized religion as Judaism was, and also because they would not worship the Emperor. So now, Constantine, as Pontiffus Maximus, usurped the Bishops, and declared himself to be the *"Vicar of Christ"* on Earth." This title was also assumed later on by the Bishops of Rome, who became the Popes.

Now, as Vicar of Christ, the Emperor, (or Pope), rules in place of Christ. With the power of the state behind him, the Emperor called a Bishops council at the city of Nicaea in the year 325 C.E. It was at this council that a unified statement of doctrine was written. All Christians were to follow it, by order of Supreme Pontiff Constantine. The day of worship was changed from the Sabbath, to Sunday. Passover was exchanged for Easter Sunday. Christmas was established as Christ's birthday. Jews were declared heretics, as were Christians who followed the Jewish forms of worship. Also Gnostic Christians were condemned. All of these trends may not have been established specifically by the Council of Nicaea, but none the less, it happened. Christianity was definably established as a religion separate from Rabbinic Judaism,(which itself had developed along side of Christianity as a result of the destruction of the Temple, and the inability to practice Biblical Judaism).

Constantine sent his mother, the Empress Helena, down to the Provence of Palestina (formerly Judea) in order to ascertain Biblical Holy sights. She practiced sorcery and divination, and it was through these methods, that she located the sights of the crucifixion, the tomb, the nativity, and other locations tied to the life of Yeshua (whom they had renamed Jesus) as well as other sights like Mount Sinai. Work was begun on churches at these locations.

Constantine was a good politician. He wanted to bring as many Romans into his church as possible, and there was need for unity across the Empire. Now that all but minor traces of the Jewish origins of the church were being stamped out, old traditions needed to be replaced with new ones. The pagans were already celebrating festivals which were adapted to the new religion. Mithra worship on *Sunday, the day of the Sun,* becomes the new Christian day of worship,

Easter(Ishtar; Astarte; Isis), who's fertility rite was celebrated close to Pesach, replaced First Fruits Day, (Yom Ha Bikkirim) and becomes a Easter Sunday, relabeled as Jesus' day of resurrection. Not all the days observed by the denominations of the modern Christianities were created by Pontiff Constantine, but he and his Bishops started these basic traditions. For three major reasons:

1. Complete Separation from Judaism
2. Imperial Unity
3. Easier Conversion of the Pagans.

However, I do believe that Constantine's conversion to what I will call, Proto-Catholicism was a sincere one. He had been a worshiper of Mithra (hence his day of worship, Sunday) before the vision, and also, a good majority of Romans were still pagans. It gained Constantine no political advantage to identify with a persecuted minority like the Christians, whose men and women of faith had been tortured, burned, hacked to pieces in Gladiatorial combat, and forced into the shadows. Nor would Constantine had taken the interest that he did in promulgating doctrine for this minority, if he had not believed himself to be sincerely converted. But his heart had not changed. Religion or not. He was still a Roman Emperor and a soldier, with the power of the Army behind his throne. I believe all of this to be true in spite of the fact that he was not baptized until very near death.

The other thing that Constantine is remembered for, is the rebuilding of the ancient Greek city of *Byzantium*,(modern Istanbul) renaming it, *Nova Roma*.(New Rome) He officially moved the capitol of the Roman Empire to the East. This ancient city, conquered by the Empire during the days of Julius Caesar, had now become the political center of its conquerors. One of his many reasons for this move, was a religious motivation. This is another reason that I believe his conversion process was sincere. Rome was still dominated by a pagan population, and ruled by a pagan senate. It was filled with pagan temples and shrines. Constantine wanted a completely new city, founded on the basis of

Concepts of Messiah

the Church. A place of church buildings and not altars to Vesta, Mars, Mithra, Saturn, Jupiter, etc,etc. The name, *New Rome* would not last long. After his death, the Romans renamed it, Constantinople(City of Constantine). It would retain this name until Muslim Turks took it in 1453, converting it by the sword to Islam. The Turkish Jihadists turned once noble church buildings into mosques, and renamed it, *Istanbul.*

The consequences of Constantine's actions led to the division of the Empire into Eastern and Western halves. The west fell apart and was taken over by the Goths, Franks, and Vandals in 476. The Eastern Roman world survived for another thousand years, and is known to us as, the *Byzantine Empire.* This division in turn led to the division of Christianity into Eastern and Western rites. Roman Catholicism emerged in the west, led by the Bishop of Rome, and the Eastern Orthodox, which until 1453, was led by the Byzantine Emperor. The Eastern Church is further divided into, Serbian, Syrian, Nestorian, Armenian, Coptic, and Russian branches. Since the passing into history of the Eastern Emperors, these are loosely guided by the Patriarch of Istanbul (Constantinople). Each branch and region is led by its own patriarchs.

In the West, the Latin rite became dominate, which is Roman Catholicism. It's administrative regions are called, **Diocese**, which again, has its origins in the Roman Empire. The Emperor Diocletian had reorganized all of the old provinces into large regional districts, which were called, Diocese. So you can see how the Catholic Church's political organization, has its origins in the governmental structure of the Western Roman Empire. These regions are ruled by Bishops. Over them are the Arch-Bishops, and then the Cardinals. Over all of these is the Pope, who is now Supreme Pontiff. Persecutions and revolution against the power of the Pope, led to the rise of the Protestant churches in their many denominations. These have further divided here in America into Evangelical groups. These include Mormons and Jehovah's witnesses, even though this is vehemently denied by the

Evangelicals such as the Baptists. I have discovered to my sadness that there is a strong prejudice against Mormon and Jehovah's witnesses by the Evangelicals who staunchly declare these two groups to be, *"cults."* Some become very offended at the very comparison. This is sad. Has not the holocaust taught us anything about where hate and bigotry can lead? Has not Islamic Terrorism shown us also where religious bigotry can ultimately lead?. If such individuals can be so against two groups which arose out of their own tradition, then it is much easier for them to extend this to Messianic Jews and the Jewish community at large. I denounce bigots everywhere, no matter what their religious or national background may be!

This history is a simple overview, in order to go into the Christianities' concept of messiah. As I said, there are key areas with which they share with Rabbinic Judaism and Messianic Judaism. More so with Messianic Judaism, but there are also key differences. It is also not the intention of this book to discuss all of the rituals of each denomination. Our interest here lies in their concepts of messiah, and specifically how this relates to the Torah. The Torah is the standard for me in this writing.

Before we start on this, I want to discuss an important difference that Christians have in regards to the messiah, as opposed to Messianic Judaism. This is the name of the messiah. To some this may seem a trivial matter. But it is far from trivial. Just as the name Easter is that of a pagan sex goddess the name of the Messiah Yeshua has been changed. Names have meaning. Names (in the Biblical context) have deep meaning and are given for a reason. One example is, *"Adam*(Ahdahm)*"* which means, *"Man."*, I am not saying that Christians use the name,*"Jesus,"* out of any sense that they are deliberately trying to worship a pagan god. Christians have inherited this from their religious tradition. Even when all this is explained to most of them, they don't care. It's their tradition of man, handed down to them from their fathers, and even Evangelicals continue this, as well as other things started by Emperor Constantine. I found the following information in the Explanatory notes in the "Scriptures" translation of the Bible, by the Institute for Scripture research, North Riding, South Africa.

Examine the name, *Jesus*. What does it mean. Consider *Iesous*, rendered as "*Jesus*" in most English translations of the New Testament up to now. For example, the authoritative Greek-English Lexicon of Liddell & Scott, under *IASO*: the Greek Goddess of healing, reveals that the name *Iaso* is Ieso in the Ionic dialect of the Greek language, *Iesous* being the genitive form. In David Kravitz, Dictionary of Greek and Roman Mythology, we find a similar form, namely *Iasus*. There were four different Greek deities with the name of *Iasus,* one of them being the Son of Rhea. Further, it is well known that *Ies* is the abbreviated form of the name *Iesous*, and Dr, Bullinger, in The Apocalypse, page 396, says *Ies* was part of the name of *Bacchus*. Also, consider looking at the book," Come Out of Her My People", written by C.J. Koster.

Isn't it curious how, even the name of the messiah gets changed as a result of Greco-Roman influence? However, there is another side to this argument, so before I condemn the Christians for using this name **Jesus**, I will give it to you. In the Septuagint, which is the very first Greek translation of the Jewish Scriptures, dating from 147 B.C.E. the name *Yehoshua* (English is Joshua) is translated as *Iesous*. This was also carried over into the New Testament. In the Tanakh, nine persons and a city have the name Yeshua, usual transliterated as "Jeshua" or "Jeshuah." This then get rendered. "Jesus," in English translations

Names are very important in the Bible, and very often reflect the character of the person to whom it was given. And this is especially true with Rabbi King Messiah. For it is said; (Matisyahu 1:18-21)

> Here is how the birth of Yeshua the Messiah took place. When his mother Miriam was engaged to Yosef, before they were married, she was found to be pregnant from the Ruach HaKodesh. Her husband-to-be, Yosef, was a man who did what is right: so he made plans to break the engagement quietly, rather than put her

to public shame. But while he was thinking about this, an angel of ADONAI appeared to him in a dream and said, "Yosef, son of David, do not be afraid to take Miriam home with you as your wife; for what has been conceived in her is from the Ruach HaKodesh. She will give birth to a son, and you are to name him Yeshua, {which means, ADONAI SAVES,'] because he will save his people from their sins.

Rabbi King Messiah has this name, because he is *the one who saves*. It is part of his character that he saves. It is his mission to save. Therefore the name, **Yeshua.** This is also the masculine form of, "*Yeshua'ah*," which means, "*Salvation*." In modern Hebrew, Yeshua's name is pronounced and written "*Yeshu*," which may have been the ancient pronunciation in the Galil. (Galilee) However, reflecting two thousand years of conflict between the Church and the Synagogue, it is also an acronym for, *"Yimach sh'mov'zikhrono"* ("May his name and memory be blotted out.") However, Yosef Vaktor, of blessed memory, a Messianic Jewish Holocaust survivor took it for a much more uplifting and positive acronym. "Yigdal sh'mo umalkhuto." ("May his name and Kingdom grow.")

The basic and simple Christian concept of messiah is, that Christ died on the cross to deal with human sin, that he was buried, that he was raised from the dead and appeared to his people—on one occasion to a group of five hundred. The resurrection is fundamental. Without it, there is no such thing as Christianity, except for the *Ger Tzaddikim, (Righteous Converts to Judaism)* the gentiles would still be pagan and there would be no need for Messianic Judaism. We would still be practicing Rabbinic Judaism, because without the resurrection, that would mean that Rabbi King Messiah has not yet come. The many attempts to explain it away fall short. In light of the scientific discoveries concerning the burial shroud at *Turin*, Italy, and the fact of the New Testament itself. This remarkable collection of 1st Century Jewish writings are a consequence of the unique and utterly different life, ministry, death and resurrection of Rabbi King Messiah.

Some people say, that all of these things came later on in Christian belief, and that over a long period of time, the ordinary Jewish Rabbi, was elevated, and eventually became known as the Son of G-d. This is the current theory in modern, Non-Messianic Jewish thinking. Through his crucifixion and resurrection, the power of Jesus the Christ (Christian terminology) was no longer limited to those people who knew him as he ministered to Israel. Now it was to be a universal and worldwide ministry

During his last *Passover Seder, (the Last Supper)* Jesus the Christ told his followers that all of G-d that they had experienced through him would continue. He thus enacted a sign using the elements of matzah and wine. The bread represented his body and the wine to be the blood of the new covenant. So the belief that G-d had manifested as a man here on earth, totally changed the world. He was still called Yeshua, his human name, but the books of the New Testament bestow upon him the highest acclaim. The acclaim being that it is he who is a reflection of G-d's glory and the exact imprint of G-d's being. For it is written by Rav Sha'ul (Apostle Paul) in Ibrim (Hebrews) 1:3;

> This Son is the radiance of the Shekhinah, the very expression of G-d's essence, upholding all that exists by his powerful word: and after he had, through him self, made purification for sins, he sat down at the right hand of HaG'dulah BaM'romim.(Greatness on high)

All these are extraordinary claims to be making about a crucified man, and the writings of the early followers, and their history, show their struggle to understand the wondrous brilliance of what had happened.

The Christians generally believe that they should follow Jesus the Christ in Baptism, which draws them into union with Christ through his death and resurrection. However, some Baptize infants. Some immerse like the Jews, while other sprinkle. Jesus the Christ transfers believers from death into life which is the free gift of G-d.

Now begins the diverging of Christians from Messianic Jews. Messianic Judaism is as firm on the Torah as is all other Judaism. That it is the unchanging law of G-d Most High, blessed be his name. That his covenant is eternal, everlasting, and unchanging. Some Evangelical Christians go part of the way on this, but stop short, attempting to separate the moral code from the ceremonial code. The Torah makes no such separation, say the Sages, Rabbis, and Elders of Israel. Groups like the Jehovah's Witnesses go as far to say that Jesus the Christ replaced the Torah with a code of Christ and claim it to be superior to the Torah. Many Evangelical groups teach the same doctrine.

Most all of the Christian denominations believe that the new covenant has set them free from the laws of the "old covenant," According to them, Jesus the Christ fulfilled the laws of the "old covenant", in the sense that to them, the word, 'fulfilled,' means that they were brought to an end. The word that Jesus speaks when he said, *"The Law and the Prophets were until John the Baptist,"* are taken to mean that the Christ has brought a new law to replace G-d's first law. This in spite of the fact that all of what the New Testament teaches, is basicly a Torah Commentary. Drawing from the writing of the Apostle Paul, they teach that the old covenant was nailed to the cross with Jesus the Christ and. that the Torah is something that is passing away. But when confronted with the fact that the crimes of rape, incest, murder and robbery are condemned by the Torah, these same people have come up with the idea that Christ nailed the ceremonial law to the cross, and that it stayed in the grave not rising with him. A fanatic young Christian, who zealously referred to the Jews as "Christ Killers," to me, also emphaticly declared that the Jewish Religion was unnecessary. All this has been taught by various Christianities over the last 1800 years or so. Not all to be sure. But let them alone! Let them believe this if they want to! If they do not keep the commandments of the LORD, out of pure intent of the heart, then it does no good for them to observe them in their flesh as a form of legalism. The Christians also draw this belief from their interpretation of Acts chapter 15. This is a dispute over whether gentile believers should observe Jewish law. The result was a compromise in which the converts would keep some basic laws and otherwise be free. The problem is, is that all of these writings have been removed from their cultural context in Judaism. What is being referred to here is the **Oral Torah** of Pharisaic Judaism, not the Torah. It was agreed that the *Traditions of the Fathers*, not be imposed upon the converts, who were coming into the Beth Yeshua, (House of Jesus) and not Beth Hillel or Bet Shammai, the two main schools of the dominate form of Pharisaic Judaism. Why should gentile converts be keeping the laws of the Pharisees? They were not being converted into that form of Judaism. The same would hold true of the doctrines of the Essenes and their, *"Works of the Law of the Community."* Gentile converts were coming into Yeshua's Judaism, not Essene Judaism, so why would you impose upon them the Traditions of the Essene Fathers? Many modern Christians are coming to this understanding, and I bless them as my brothers and sisters in Messiah Yeshua. But I do not seek to force through condemnation, any Gentile who does not feel convicted in his heart, to walk the path of a Messianic Jew. All who are sincere are welcome. Those who are not, worship in peace, as your free will dictates.

What is the meaning of "Church?" It's meaning is, *"Convocation"* According to generally accepted Christian doctrine, the Church is the designated assembly of those people whom G-d convokes, ie, gathers together to form the People of G-d, and who themselves, being nourished within and with the body of Christ, become the body of Christ. This concept of messiah removes from him an earthly body and an earthly Kingdom, and spiritualizes it as something that his happening now. That the Church is the Kingdom of Heaven on earth. This teaching is prevalent within Roman Catholicism. This means that the Church is the mystical body of Christ. She is one, yet formed of two components, divine and human. This is a mystery, and Christians can only accept it with faith.

The Church is the sacrament of salvation in the world, and is the sign and the instrument of the communion with G-d. They believe that the Church is both the means and the goal of the LORD's plan. A plan prefigured in creation, prepared for in the old covenant, and founded by the ministry of Jesus Christ. The *plan of salvation* was then fulfilled by his redemptive sacrifice on the cross and his resurrection. They believe that the Church is the manifestation of salvation on earth, empowered by the outpouring of the Holy Spirit ,and will thus be perfected in the glory of heaven as the great assembly of all the Christians on earth. The Catholics teach that the Church's first purpose is to be the sacrament—a sign and and instrument of communion with G-d and thus unity among all mankind.

The concept of messiah that all Christians share is that Jesus the Christ is the mystery of salvation. On this, all the denominations spread over the length and breadth of the entire world, find common ground. They may disagree on a great many things, but on this concept of messiah, they are all in full agreement. St Augustine declared; that there was no other mystery of G-d, except Christ.

Each denomination seems to add things to the basic concept, teaching grace coupled with works and baptism in water, and the Holy Spirit in order to receive salvation. Many in Roman Catholicism teach that those who do not adhere to their denomination, and accept the authority of the Pope, are not saved and will go to hell. In modern times under the new Catechism this has been changed to a form that is more acceptable and tolerant of other Christianities and other religions. The teaching now is that in all nations, anyone who fears G-d and does what is right is acceptable to G-d. This is a startling turn of events! If Jesus Christ is the atonement, but still Pagans and Muslims who do not accept him can still get in—then for what did he die? Evangelical groups in no way accept this doctrine, nor do Jehovah's Witnesses and Mormons.

.

As you know by now, that the general Christian concept of messiah, is that he is much more than merely the King of Israel, the Son of

David, but the Son of G-d. The Christians believe in a doctrine called the,"*Trinity,*" or , "*Triune G-d*" consisting of G-d the Father; G-d the Son, and G-d the Holy Spirit. The mystery of one G-d in three Persons They believe that the revealed truth of the *Holy Trinity* is at the root of the Church's living faith. But the mystery of the Trinity in itself is inaccessible to the human mind. It is the object of pure faith in that it was revealed for the first time by Jesus the Christ, who is the divine Son of the Eternal Father.

Christian Trinitarian doctrine is thus; I have drawn this from the new Roman Catholic Catechism.

G-d the Father;

G-d the Father is the first Person of the Holy Trinity. Jesus the Christ revealed that G-d is a unique Father. He is not just the creator of all things, but is the eternal and heavenly Father of his only begotten Son, who is con-substantial with the Father.

G-d the Son;

Jesus the Christ: The eternal Son of G-d who was born of the Virgin Mary, suffered crucifixion and then rose again on the third day. Afterwords he ascended into heaven to sit at the right hand of the Father. At at the end of the ages, he will return again to judge the living and the dead.

G-d the Holy Spirit;

The third Person of the Holy Trinity. Also called the Advocate, and the Spirit of Truth. He is at work with the Father and the Son from the beginning to the end of the divine plan of salvation. And it is by his drawing that one comes to know Jesus the Christ as Lord and Savior, and by his inspiration that is the fountain head of prophecy, and of the writing of the Holy Scriptures.

I will point out that this doctrine is misunderstood by Jews and Muslims, who see it as the worship of three different gods. I understand this in light of what has been taught by the Jewish Mystics in the Zohar, concerning the seferot. These are the aspects of the divine personality of G-d., however this is not the place to start a detailed explanation of this. Suffice is to say, that I believe that the trinity doctrine developed from the way that Rabbi King Messiah used to relate to mankind, the nature of G-d.. A way that we could better understand, the all encompassing nature of G-d, who ultimately is Ein Sof. This term means *"There is no end."* that which is boundless; the infinite. The ultimate reality of G-d beyond all specific qualities that man can grasp. G-d beyond G-d. So I believe that the Trinity is just a part of the aspects of G-d, the *Seferot,* that the Blessed Holy One, has allowed us to view. There are other passages of scripture in Hisgalus (Revelation) which refer to G-d in terms of *seven-fold spirits. This* verse does not mean that Hashem is seven beings in a G-d head as the Trinity does not mean that there are three beings in a Godhead. I have attached an appendix to this writing in order to explain my own understanding of this idea. Do not put G-d in a box. He's too big! I will say to the Christians, the same thing I say to the Rabbinic Jews. Never say, never, when it comes to G-d. He is bigger than all our creeds doctrines and dogmas. I agree with what was written by Sir William Shakespeare when he wrote;

> "There are more things in heaven and earth, Horatio, than are dreamed of in your philosophies."

Next I want to deal with the doctrine of the Virgin Mary, which is held specifically by the Roman Catholic Church. I must relate it because it is a key component in their concept of messiah, which is what this book is all about. My information is drawn from their *Catechism*. I will not quote it verbatim but will just summarize what it teaches. The fact that the Messiah Yeshua was born from a virgin is not in dispute. All Christians, and even Messianic Judaism is in agreement with this, because G-d himself said that it would be so, in Scripture. What is in dispute, is the nature of the woman herself and her later roll in life, and now.

What Catholicism believes about her is tied into what it believes about Jesus the Christ, and what it teaches about her shines a light, in turn on its faith in Jesus the Christ. They believe that she was pre-destined to form in her womb the fleshly body of the Son of G-d, but only with her free cooperation. She gave her consent to be the, **"Mother of G-d."** In order to become the mother of the Savior she had to be enriched by G-d with all the appropriate gifts that she would need in order to carry out the task at hand. So G-d filled her with grace. She was redeemed from the very moment that she was conceived and this is the doctrine of the immaculate conception. This was proclaimed by Pope Pius IX in 1854:

> The most blessed Virgin Mary was, from the first moment of her conception, by a singular grace and privilege of almighty G-d and by virtue of the merits of Jesus Christ, Savior of the human race, preserved immune from all stain of original sin.(New Roman Catholic Catechism)

Catholics believe that Mary was endowed with the glory of a unique holiness from the very moment her parents conceived her. This enrichment comes wholly from Christ and she is redeemed in a more exalted manner by reason of her Son. She is more blessed by the Father than any created person. The Catholic Church confesses that Mary is truly the **"Mother of G-d."** They believe that she remained a perpetual virgin, even in the act of giving birth to Jesus the Christ, and in fact, his birth, far from diminishing his mother's virginal integrity, gave it greater sanctification. Catholic liturgy celebrates her as, *"Aeiparthenos,* or, *"Ever-virgin."* They believe that Jesus was her only son, and that the brothers and sisters of Jesus the Christ, mentioned by the Bible, were only close relations according to old testament tradition. They teach that Yeshua's brothers and sisters were the children of another Mary, probably the sister of Eleazar (Lazarus).In light of my knowledge of traditional Judaism, I do not accept this idea..

The Eastern Orthodox refer to Mary as, *'The All-Holy (Panagia)* and celebrate her as sin free, formed by the Holy Spirit and formed as a new creature. By G-d's grace, Mary was completely sin free her entire life. [My belief, is that all of this is a continuation of the pagan traditions of the ancient near east, who worshiped a goddess known as the "Queen of Heaven." She had a son by the name of Simmeramus. The Scriptures declare in no uncertain terms that we are never to worship the Queen of Heaven.] The Catholic concept of messiah, and the Eastern Orthodox, includes the belief that Jesus the Christ established *seven sacraments*, or, *mysteries*;

1. Baptism,
2. Conformation,
3. Eucharist,
4. Penance,
5. Anointing of the sick
6. Holy Orders,
7. Matrimony.

Out of all of these, I am going to deal only with the **Eucharist,** because it is more specific to their concept of messiah than all of the others. Eucharist is the ritual which constitutes the principle celebration of, and communion in the paschal mystery of Jesus the Christ. It is also known as the; *Holy Sacrifice of the Mass.* It is celebrated on Sunday and is the heart and soul of life in the Catholic Church as well as the Eastern Orthodox Rites. *Canon of of the Mass,* which is also known as the *Eucharistic Prayer,* contains the Prayer of Thanksgiving and consecration. The Church believes that the wine is actually transformed into the blood of Jesus the Christ, and the bread wafers into his flesh. This in fulfillment of his words that he spoke as. [I am using his Christian name now] recorded in the book of Yochanan (John)

Jesus therefore said to them, "Truly, truly, I say unto you, unless you eat the flesh of the Son of Man and drink his blood, you possess no life in yourselves. [Yochanan (John)chapter 6: 53]

The Evangelical, Charismatic, Protestant, and Non-Denominational Church groups, do not accept the Eucharist at all. Their celebration of communion is done in remembrance of Jesus the Christ and what he did on the cross. They do not believe that his flesh and blood are sacramentally present in the wine and bread. While it is still not a true Passover Seder in the Messianic Jewish sense, it is much closer to it than the Eucharist.

Before closing out this chapter I will relate two other concepts of messiah from two other groups, which are part of the Christian denominational groupings, but are vehemently denied as such by the Evangelicals. In fact there is much prejudice and intolerance among the Evangelicals against these people, to whom they refer to as, *"Cults"*. These definitions are just extremely brief and are just simple expressions of where they stand when it comes to Jesus the Christ. My Evangelical friends are going to be upset when they read this, because I have grouped the Mormons and Jehovah's Witnesses under the title, Christian. However, I believe that they are, because they arose out of the Western Christian Protestant tradition.

Mormons

The Mormon Concept of Messiah is generally the same as other Christian groups however they do have defining beliefs and practices which set them vastly apart from other Christians. So much so that there is extreme prejudice by many Evangelicals against the Mormons, whom they define as a cult.

The Mormon doctrine of salvation comes in two parts: general and individual. They believe that all of mankind will be saved at the final resurrection and will be judged by their works. If a person wants to earn forgiveness from personal sins, he must have faith in Jesus the Christ, baptism by immersion, obedience to Mormon doctrine, good works, and keeping G-d's commandments.

The following material is from the LDS Newsroom website, Http://www.mormonnewsroom.org which has a complete and detailed list of what the Mormon concept of Messiah is

Latter-day Saints are Christians on the basis of our doctrine, our defined relationship to Christ, our patterns of worship and our way of life.

What *Do* We Believe About Christ?

- We believe Jesus is the Son of God, the Only Begotten Son in the flesh (John 3:16). We accept the prophetic declarations in the Old Testament that refer directly and powerfully to the coming of the Messiah, the Savior of all humankind. We believe that Jesus of Nazareth was and is the fulfillment of those prophecies.

- We believe the accounts of Jesus' life and ministry recorded in Matthew, Mark, Luke and John in the New Testament to be historical and truthful. For us the Jesus of history is indeed the Christ of faith. While we do not believe the Bible to be inerrant, complete or the final word of God, we accept the essential details of the Gospels and more particularly the divine witness of those men who walked and talked with Him or were mentored by His chosen apostles.

- We believe that He was born of a virgin, Mary, in Bethlehem of Judea in what has come to be known as the meridian of time, the central point in salvation history. From His mother, Mary, Jesus inherited mortality, the capacity to feel the frustrations and ills of this world, including the capacity to die. We believe that Jesus was fully human in that He was subject to sickness, to pain and to temptation.

- We believe Jesus is the Son of God the Father and as such inherited powers of godhood and divinity from His Father, including immortality, the capacity to live forever. While He walked the dusty road of Palestine as a man, He possessed the powers of a God and ministered as one

Concepts of Messiah

having authority, including power over the elements and even power over life and death.

- We believe Jesus performed miracles, including granting sight to the blind, hearing to the deaf, life to some who had died and forgiveness to those steeped in sin. We believe the New Testament accounts of healings and nature miracles and the cleansing of human souls to be authentic and real.

- We believe Jesus taught His gospel — the glad tidings or good news that salvation had come to earth through Him — in order that people might more clearly understand both their relationship to God the Father and their responsibility to each other.

- We believe Jesus selected leaders, invested them with authority and organized a church. We maintain that the Church of Jesus Christ was established, as the Apostle Paul later wrote, for the perfection and unity of the saints (Ephesians 4:11–14).

- We believe that Jesus' teachings and His own matchless and perfect life provide a pattern for men and women to live by and that we must emulate that pattern as best we can to find true happiness and fulfillment in this life.

- We believe Jesus suffered in the Garden of Gethsemane and that He submitted to a cruel death on the cross of Calvary, all as a willing sacrifice, a substitutionary atonement for our sins. That offering is made efficacious as we exercise faith and trust in Him; repent of our sins; are baptized by immersion as a symbol of our acceptance of His death, burial and rise to newness of life; and receive the gift of the Holy Ghost (Acts 2:37–38; 3 Nephi 27:19–20). While no one of us can comprehend how and in what manner one person can take upon himself the effects of the sins of another — or, even more mysteriously, the sins of all men and women — we accept and glory in the transcendent reality that Christ remits our sins through His suffering. We know it is true because we have experienced it personally. Further, we believe that He died, was buried and rose from the dead and that His resurrection was a physical reality. We believe that the effects of His rise from the tomb pass upon all men and women. "As in Adam all die, even so in Christ shall all be made alive" (Corinthians 15:22).

- We do not believe that we can either overcome the flesh or gain eternal reward through our own unaided efforts. We must work to our limit and then rely upon the merits, mercy and grace of the Holy One of Israel to see us through the struggles of life and into life eternal (2 Nephi 31:19; Moroni 6:4). We believe that while human works are necessary— including exercising faith in Christ, repenting of our sins, receiving the sacraments or ordinances of salvation and rendering Christian service to our neighbors — they are not sufficient for salvation (2 Nephi 25:23; Moroni 10:32). We believe that our discipleship ought to be evident in the way we live our lives.

Jesus Christ is the central figure in the doctrine and practice of *The Church of Jesus Christ of Latter-day Saints*. He is the Redeemer. He is the prototype of all saved beings, the standard of salvation. Jesus explained that "no man cometh unto the Father, but by me" (John 14:6). We acknowledge Jesus Christ as the source of truth and redemption, as the light and life of the world, as the way to the Father (John 14:6; 2 Nephi 25:29; 3 Nephi 11:11). We worship Him in that we look to Him for deliverance and redemption and seek to emulate His matchless life (D&C 93:12–20). Truly, as one Book of Mormon prophet proclaimed, "We talk of Christ, we rejoice in Christ, we preach of Christ, ... that our children may know to what source they may look for a remission of their sins" (2 Nephi 25:26).

As to whether we worship a "different Jesus," we say again: We accept and endorse the testimony of the New Testament writers. Jesus is the promised Messiah, the resurrection and the life (John 11:25), literally the light of the world (John 8:12). Everything that testifies of His divine birth, His goodness, His transforming power and His godhood, we embrace enthusiastically. But we also rejoice in the additional knowledge latter-day prophets have provided about our Lord and Savior. President Brigham Young thus declared that we, the Latter-day Saints, take the liberty of believing more than our Christian brethren: we not only believe ... the Bible, but ... the whole of the plan of salvation that Jesus has given to us. Do we differ from others who believe in the Lord Jesus Christ? No, only in believing more.[x]

It is the "more" that makes many in the Christian world very nervous and usually suspicious of us. But it is the "more" that allows us to make a significant contribution in the religious world. Elder Boyd K. Packer observed: "We do not claim that others have no truth. ... Converts to the Church may bring with them all the truth they possess and have it added upon.

Jehovah's Witnesses.

Jehovah's Witnesses believe in the absolute unity of G-d. They do not believe in the Trinity like other Christians. Their concept of messiah is; that Jesus the Christ is the Son of G-d, but is inferior to G-d. They do not believe that he was resurrected bodily, but only as a spirit. They believe that a person works for his own salvation, through the death of Jesus the Christ. Their concept of messiah teaches also that Jesus the Christ returned to earth in 1914, but returned to heaven, and now rules from there. They also believe that Jesus the Christ brought and end to the Torah and replaced it with a "Code of Christ," which is superior to the Laws of Moses. Jehovah's Witnesses do not believe in the immortality of the soul, and view that doctrine as something the Jews adopted from Greco-Roman paganism. They are harshly critical of any form of Judaism or any of our Talmudic Laws.

Here is a short summary from Wikipedia concerning their concept of messiah;

Jehovah's Witnesses emphasize use of God's biblical name, represented in the original texts by the Tetragramaton, and in English they prefer to use the name, *Jehovah* They believe that Jehovah is the only true God, the creator of all things, and the *"Universal Sovereign"*. They believe that all worship should be directed toward him, and that he is not part of a Trinity consequently, the religion places more emphasis on God than on Christ. They believe that the Holy Spirit is God's power or "active force" rather than a person.

Jehovah's Witnesses believe that Jesus is God's only direct creation, that everything else was created by means of Christ, and that the initial unassisted act of creation uniquely identifies Jesus as God's "only-begotten Son". Jesus served as a redeemer and a ransome sacrifice to pay for the sins of humankind. They believe Jesus died on a single upright torture stake rather than the traditional cross They believe that references in the Bible to the Archangel Michael, Abaddon(Apollyon), and ,"the word," all refer to Jesus. Jesus is considered to be the only intercessor and high priest between God and humankind, and appointed by God as the king and judge of his kingdom. His role as a mediator (referred to in 1 Timothy 2:5) is applied to the 'anointed' class, though the 'other sheep' are said to also benefit from the arrangement.

Summary

The summary of this chapter is an overview of the concepts of messiah that I feel represent most Christian beliefs. First the Bible. It is the inspired and written word of G-d. It is his message of love to all mankind. It is a divine message system that is, from beyond our space-time continuum. G-d is all seeing, all knowing, all powerful all just, and all loving. That G-d is eternal and exists in three persons; Father, Son, and Holy Spirit. That the Son is Jesus the Christ who was born of the Virgin Mary is fully G-d, and fully He is the way, the truth and the life. No one goes to the Father except by him, because of his atonement sacrifice of himself on the cross. That he claimed the authority of G-d, and is the fulfillment of all the prophetic expectations of both old and new testaments. That Jesus the Christ died in our place as the perfect substitute and perfect sacrifice for sin. Jesus the Christ is the perfect mediator between G-d and man and the perfect *Priest-King,* That Jesus the Christ was bodily raised from the dead on the third day. Because of this, all who call upon his name, and except him into their lives as Lord and King, are freely given the gift of eternal life. Life eternal, because the Bible teaches that the souls of men are immortal and that Jesus the Christ has given his people this great inheritance. Believers will be with him through all eternity in heaven where we shall have access to G-d. And the final abode of those who reject Jesus the Christ, is an eternal hell, living apart from G-d. Christians teach that hell is a place of eternal torment and punishment. Outer darkness and the lake of fire. That at the end of days, Jesus the Christ shall return to earth to rule and reign for a thousand years. A time in which Satan and his hosts will be locked away in the Abyss.

The concept of the Church is so very special and very important to Christianity, because G-d has purchased the Church with the blood of Christ.

Finally, the Lord's Supper. Messianic Jews believe that this is part and parcel of the traditional Jewish *Seder.* That nothing new was initiated. We believe that Rabbi King Messiah brought the Passover celebration to its greater understanding in meaning, which according to scripture, is one of the key missions of Rabbi King Messiah. To give a more perfect interpretation of the Torah. However, most Christians have detached it from its Jewish roots. They believe that they should only celebrate communion, and most don't do this during Passover, but any time of the year. For me, that is sad. Their Messiah was a Jew. The most observant Religious Jew in all of history .Strive to do as he did. The Christian view of the Lord's supper, is that he introduced it on the night before he was crucified, and he instructed his followers to observe it until his return. To the Catholics and the Eastern Rites, this has become the Eucharist. To most others, it involves a looking back to the historical event of the death of the Messiah. The bread is a symbol of his body, offered as a sacrifice. The blood is symbolized by a cup of wine. Blood that was shed for forgiveness of sins. Only those who know him as Lord and savior should participate in the Lord's supper, and is an occasion for spiritual growth.

This brings to a close this chapter, Jesus the Christ. I am sure that a lot of what I have brought out will answer some questions, and raise many more. I hope that the reader finds this information enlightening and informative.

Mochiach Ha Chaim Torah

(Messiah The Living Torah)

Back in the introduction, I brought up a concept which I refer to as, **Living Torah**. I dealt with this subject matter in the book that titled, **Torah Is Calling.** However, it is a concept of messiah, which cannot be overlooked.. Why did I wait until the last chapter to deal with this? It is because it is a triumph. The Messianic Jews and the Christians believe that Yeshua Ha Notzri was, and is to come. He is referred to as, *"The Word."* This can also be translated as *"Torah,"* and even as He is alive, his word is living. Not only is He; Mochiach ben Dovid; Mochiach ben Yosef, and Mochiach ben Elohim, he is Mochiach Chaim Torah. He is our triumph!

A few years ago, I was reading the debates between some Rabbis. *"How far back before creation did the Torah exist?"* This seems confusing, in light of the fact that the 613 instructions and commandments were not given in a written form until the revelation at Sinai. The uninformed may think that these Rabbis were just debating nonsense and legend. Not so! This is no legend! It is fact! The Rabbis were very wise and learned men, who spent most of their lives searching the scriptures. They have found layer upon layer of hidden meaning, under the Hebrew words of which the Bible is composed, even down to the very letters themselves. Modern Rabbis engage in this type of study. Messianic Jewish Rabbi John Popp did a series of teachings called, "The Hebrew Letter Series." It was quite revealing.

Once more, the great Rabbis of history like Moses Maimonides discovered that the Torah had equal distant letter sequencing codes. (ELS) This has become very popular these days, because of the advent of the super computer. These programs, developed in Israel scan the text of the Torah finding these codes, showing us how incredible the scriptures realy are. No mortal man could conspire to develop such a vast coding system like we find in the Tanakh. This is why the Rabbis of the Talmud always said that the entire history of mankind is contained in the Torah These codes are only found in the canonized Hebrew books. This is the imprint of G-d upon them.

Concerning the *B'rit Hadashah* (The New Testament). I don't know if anyone has started the development of a program to search in it for ELS codes, but I really hope that they do. Just like the Tanakh, it is composed in structures of sevens. This is what is referred to as a. **"Heptatic Structure."** I have no doubt that the writings of the B'rit Hadashah are G-d breathed. They were written by the inspired hands of the first Messianic Rabbis.

By all of this, we have learned that the scriptures are indeed, the words of the living G-d. Now, if these are His words, then they have always been in the mind of G-d. Remember, the Ancient Holy One, blessed be He, is not subject to this universe in which we live. His abode is above and beyond the space-time continuum, and we refer to it as, *eternity*. This means that the Torah is just as eternal as G-d. So this debate is easily solved, as to how far back before creation the Torah reaches.

Just what is this concept of messiah? Why do I refer to him as, **"Messiah The Living Torah"** [Ha Mochiach Chaim Torah. (Chaim, pronounced, Hai-eem)] Look at the book of Proverbs chapter 8. Here it speaks of wisdom. **Hokhmah**. This is one of the ten aspects of G-d, or Crowns, also called, "*Sefirot*", that we may know. The hokhmah of which it speaks is in reference to the written Torah. The Bible is always consistent throughout from beginning to beginning. Why do I say, beginning to beginning? Because even the end is the birth of a new beginning. Life everlasting. Turning into the B'rit Hadashah, to the Besuras Hageulah of Yochanan (Gospel of John). The very first chapter begins very much like the Torah. In fact the very first word is the same." B'reshite" In the beginning." Look closely at it, and then re-translate, D'var, (Word) to Torah.(law, instructions) I write it now with this change;

> In the beginning was the *Torah*, and the *Torah* was with G-d and the Torah was G-d. He was with G-d in the beginning. All things came to be through Him, and without him, nothing made had

being. In Him was life and the life was the light of mankind. The light shines in the darkness and the darkness has not suppressed it. There was a man sent from G-d whose name was Yochanan. He came to be a testimony. To bear witness concerning the light; so that through him, everyone might put his trust in G-d and be faithful to him. He himself was not that light; no, he came to bear witness concerning the light. This was the true light, which gives light to everyone entering the world. He was in the world—the world came to be through him—yet the world did not know him. He came to his own, and his own people were not accepting. But as many as receive him as Messiah, to them he gave the validity to become in fact the children of G-d. The *Torah* became a human and lived with us, and we saw his shekinah, the shekinah of the Father's only son, full of grace and truth. Yochanan witnessed concerning him when he cried out, "This is the man I was talking about when I said, 'He who comes after me is really before me in priority, because before I came to be, he was. We have all received from the fullness of him, grace upon grace. For giving of the *Torah* was graciously bestowed through Moshe Rabbeinu, but grace and truth of G-d came through Messiah Yeshua. No one has ever seen G-d; but the only and unique Son, who is identical with G-d and as at the Father's side--he has made him known.

This is very much like the mystical writing found in the Zohar. Dare I say that the Rabbi that wrote this, Yochanan Ha Shliach (John the Apostle) was himself a mystic of the first order. His writings show this to be the case. Examine this very deep, Zoharic-like concept of messiah, which Hashem has revealed to us through Yochanan Ha Shliach, concerning the nature of the messiah. It explains that messiah is the first form of Torah, The Living Torah! And how the Holy One, blessed be his name, stepped out of the realm of eternity, and came into the *Olam Hazeh* (this present world/universe) which he had created, dwelling among us.

In the chapter, Mochiach ben Elohim, it was my intention to bring out this concept of messiah from the Tanakh, without referencing the B'rit Hadashah. This for the benefit of those would think that this concept of messiah is only a New Testament thing. Not so. Now we see how our Messianic Jewish ancestors gloried in this, giving it to the world. We saw how this was adapted by the Christianities. Now we come back to it in the mystical writings of Yochanan Ha Shliach, where he is teaching us that Rabban Yeshua is; *Messiah the Living Torah*.

I will continue to draw lessons from the Besuras Hageulah of Yochanan. Rabbi King Messiah appeared in a vision to Natan'el. Mochiach soon afterwords. came to the future Messianic Jewish Rabbi and called him out in honor, declaring him to be a man in whom no deceit was found.

Natan'el said to him 'From where do you know me?" Yeshua answered and said to him, "Before Phillipos called you, when you were under the fig tree, I saw you." Natan'el answered and said unto him, "Rabbi, you are the Son of G-d. You are the King of Israel.

Rabbi Natan'el responded in this manner, because I believe that he had been in morning prayers wearing his talit and teffillin. He immediately recognized Rabban Yeshua as the one in the vision from heaven. This is why he made the declaration in such an up front and matter of fact manner. Shimon Kefa (Peter) Phillipos and Andrew must have been quite startled.

To further illustrate the point, I have chosen another section from Yochanan's book. Rabbi King Messiah was debating with a group of people in the treasury room of the Beit Hamikdash.(The Temple) He was trying to explain to them a great many things. He used very strong language

"You are of your Father the Devil."[Yochanan 8:44a]

This group was probably some Prushim (Pharisee) of the School of Shammai. The term that Rabbi King Messiah used against them, was identical with what Rabbi Hillel had said concerning Bet Shammai. Hillel was founder of the School of Prushim which bore his name. Hillel was also from the family of King David, but from a different branch than Rabbi King Messiah. At the end of this debate, Yeshua the Messiah said;

> Abraham your father was glad that he would see my day;then he saw it and was glad." "Why, you're not yet fifty years old," the Judeans relied; "and you have seen Avraham?"Yeshua replied, "Before Avraham was, I AM." At this they picked up stones to throw at him; but Yeshua was hidden and left the Temple Precinct. [Yochanan 8:56-59;]

This gathering of Prushim may have been among the very best Torah scholars in all Israel. But even these learned scholars had no advanced scientific knowledge of the kind that G-d has graciously allowed modern man to learn. They had no concept of the physical properties of the space-time continuum. They knew nothing of the fabric of space, and how Hashem can enter and exit at any point in the timeline that he chooses. This is one of the ways that the Ancient Holy One, blessed be His Name, could see Avraham. YHVH is almighty and eternal. We know from the story of Eleazar the beggar and the rich noble, that Avraham Aveinu was alive as a living spirit in paradise. Avraham did indeed get to witness the advent of *Messiah the Living Torah*. It would have done no further good for Rabbi King Messiah to explain the concept to them. For as he said ;

> "I have told you of earthy things and you do not understand. How then will you understand the things of heaven."[Yochanan 3:12]

This is indeed the triumph of triumphs. That the word of the Ancient Holy One, blessed be His name, has tabernacled among men. Such a powerful doctrine is embodied in this small passage of scripture. Rabbi King Messiah is the way, the truth, and the life. *Mochiach Chaim Torah.*

In another of his writings, Yochanan says something very similar. He is illustrating the same wonderful concept of messiah, that is embodied in the titles, **Mochiach ben Elohim,** and **Ha Mochiach Chaim Torah.**

> What was from the beginning, what we have heard, what we have seen with our eyes, what we have looked upon, and our hands have handled, concerning the word of life. And the life was manifested, and we have seen, and bear witness, and announce to you that everlasting life which was with the Father and manifested to us. [1st Yochanan 1: 1-2;]

Here is is again,"*word of life.*" This is the Living Torah. His words are life. **D'var Chaim**. This was what was ,"from the beginning," As it is said in B'reshite 1:1a

"In the beginning G-d."

Before that there is only G-d, who withdrew part of himself in order that we might live. *"And the life was manifested."* This is Rabbi King Messiah. For G-d has walked among us. And, *"everlasting life which was with the Father."* This tells us that Yeshua the Messiah has always existed with and is part of the Father. One of the crowns of which we are given to know, because it says, "manifested to us.

What shall be the end of these things, in order that there might be a new beginning? It is said, again by Yochanan Ha Shliach;

> "Out of his mouth went a sharp two-edged sword"[Hisgalus (Revelation) 1-16b;]

Why? Because his words are as a sword with two edges, cutting at both sides. Cutting away with the sound of his voice, all which is evil, and yet, dubbing as Knights, those who freely bind themselves as bond-servants to his heavenly throne. Mochiach Chaim Torah, may he return, swiftly and soon in our lifetimes, for all of us inscribed in Sefer Chaim.(Book of Life)

Conclusion.

What are we to draw from everything in this book? That though men have many concepts of messiah, there is only one Rabbi King Messiah. We have gone through the major concepts of messiah that are prevalent on the world scene today. Islamic, Rabbinic and Messianic Jewish, and Christian. Then we dealt with deepest one last, which is not so well understood. I'm sure that there is much more to write about the concepts of messiah, should the Blessed Holy One give inspiration for such works.

The only concept of messiah that I feel is a real and present danger, are those of Sunni and Shi'ite Islam. I believe that when the Mahdi arrives on the scene, he will be what is known as; **The Beast.** The False Messiah! He who is Ant-Messiah! He will lead all Islam on a global jihad, utilizing open field warfare and weapons of mass destruction. A nuclear nightmare, from who only the timely arrival of Yeshua Ha Notzri as Mochiach ben Dovid can save us. It will not be this low scale terrorist campaign which is now being waged by the likes of Al Qaeda, the Taliban, Muslim Brotherhood, Hamas, and the Hezbollah. (The Hezbos is I like to call them) No, the style of the Mahdi will be a real world war to crush all other religions and political systems. But then we shall see the return of Mochiach ben Dovid!He will stop the Mahdi, casting him into Geh-hinnom, right along with Allah (Satan). Then shall be fulfilled that which was spoken by Yochanan ha hatvil (John the Baptist;

> "HIS WINNOWING FORK IS IN HIS HAND, AND HE SHALL THOUGHLY CLEANSE HIS THRESHING-FLOOR, AND GATHER HIS WHEAT INTO THE STOREHOUSE, BUT THE CHAFF HE SHALL BURN WITH UNQUENCHABLE FIRE!"

I wish to thank Pete and Dawn Charabaneau very much. At the start of this writing, I was in a major transition in my life. Getting ready for my return home to Carlsbad, New Mexico. Pete and Dawn have always been there for me, and have provided a shelter. An oasis to come back to, and a quiet, serene place in which to compose my writings, to read, contemplate, and to pray. For these wonderful people who walk the path of Torah I give you this scripture as a blessing; D'varim 7:6;

> For you are a set-apart people to YHVH your G-d has chosen you to be a people for himself, a treasured possession above all the peoples on the face of the earth.

May you be inscribed into the book of life.

Amen.
Signed: Yehoiakin ben Ya'ocov.

Appendix I
Islam in Bible Prophecy

Symbolic Horses

The *Green horse of the Apocalypse* was a terrible Prophetic vision. In the book of Hisgalus (Rev) the Shliach (Apostle) Yochanan (John) witnessed the Day of the Lord. Part of his visioned echoed back to that of the Prophet Zakarya, who had witnessed these same symbols. However Yochanan, specifically witnessed a Green Horse It is my belief, that each one of these Horses represents periods of time and political systems. Hisgalus Chapter 6 discusses first a white horse,then another of fiery red, then another of black, the rider of which is holding a pair of scales. The others had been holding weapons. This one is concerned about commodities and wages. Then look what happens. Starting in verse 7 and going to 11;

> And when he opened the fourth seal, I heard a voice from the fourth living creature saying, "Come!" And I looked, and behold, a pale green horse, and the one seated on it {was named} Death, and Hades followed after him. And authority was granted to them over a fourth of the earth, to kill by the sword and by famine and by pestilence and by the wild beasts of the earth. And when he opened the fifth seal, I saw under the altar the souls of those who had been slaughtered because of the word of God and because of the testimony which they had, and they cried out with a loud voice, saying, "{How long}, holy and true Lord, will you not judge and avenge our blood from those who live on the earth?" And to each one of them a white robe was given, and it was said to them that they should rest yet a short time, until [the number of] their fellow slaves and their brothers who were about to be killed as they [had been] were completed also. (LEB)

Here is what I believe passionately. The first one is white. This represents both the *League of Nations,* and it's successor, the *United*

Nations. They have troops which are armed, and yet they ride around in white vehicles. White symbolizes peace! They have not brought peace! It services dictators and tyrants! Look at the wicked nations which have served on the so-called human rights commission! The likes of China and Libya to name a couple! Muslim states who are guilty of the worst human rights violations and bigotry have their say and are given equality with free nations like the USA, Canada, and Israel! The United Nations on its White Horse ushered in the age of the *Red Horse!*

The end of the rule of the Czars in Russia during the final years of the First World War, brought the rise of the Soviet Union, symbolized by the *red flag*. This inaugurated two generations of wars across the globe under the guise of peoples liberation movements. The result was that millions have been slaughtered. The most horrific Red Horse of them all was Nazi Germany. They were fanatic left wing Socialists under a flag of *genocide*. The black swastika on *red flags*! Imperial Japan with its symbol of the *red sun* rising in the east. The end of the Second World War in the flames of a nuclear nightmare did not end the cycle of the Red Horse. He was soon riding across China with *Mao Zedong* sitting upon his back. *Communism* spread across eastern Europe and Southeast Asia. The Red Horse rode across Africa and left hoof prints in Cuba and Latin America. Red is also the Socialist economic system.

In the same time period, came the *Black Horse.* This represents the capitalist economic system and symbolizes the unity of the globalized economy. Look at all of our recent financial meltdowns as the rich get richer and the poor are dragged through the dirt and kept in grinding poverty by the greed of evil government taxes and fascist corporations, who set up sweat shops in impoverished nations and pay the poor workers penny wages! Our tax dollars have gone to bail out mega financiers who set astride the *Black Horse*, while they come after the low income people with harassing debt collectors with no pity! *The Black Horse of the Apocalypse!*

It was like a dream come true for me. In the early 1990s, the Soviet Union fell apart. I had been stationed in the 1980s in Fulda, Germany, with the 11th Armored Cavalry Regiment. I was assigned to Border Operations at Observation Post Alpha, which was along the East German Border, just above and a little east of the village of Rasdorf. I drove patrol jeeps up and down many miles of the Inter-German Border. A Wall of steel, and razor wire fences, guarded by towers every few miles. Dog runs containing the most vicious German Shepherd dogs that you can imagine. The East German Border Guards had been given a," **shoot-to-kill order**," regarding any of their fellow citizens of the so-called, German Democratic Republic who might attempt to cross this barrier. This was the face of communism that I could see every day and it was gray and ugly. Then in the early nineties, all of it caved in. The most heavily armed Empire that has ever existed on the face of the earth, imploded in on itself. Eastern Europe is still recovering from the oppression of the Red Horse. The Red Horse is still kicking around in China, Southeast Asia, and in Cuba and Venezuela, but it is not the menace that it once was.

The time of the Red Horse has passed, and we have now entered into that of the **Green Horse**. The 3rd Jihad of Islam. This Horse was born as a foal in 1979, when the clerics seized power in Iran, which is the old *Persian Empire*. Warning signs of this were all around us. The fanatic bigotry of the Arabs against the Jewish people was fueled during World War II by the Nazis! During the early stages of the Arab attacks against the reborn nation of Israel, these wars were part of the Red Horse. The regimes in the Arab States were socialist and secular. Rulers like Gamal Abdul Nasser of Egypt, was a Socialist who oppressed Islamic movements.

The 1979 Islamic Revolution in Iran brought about something new. Muslim opposition to Israel and the west was no longer a Socialist vs Capitalist struggle. It became a religious one; a **Jihad.** *Suicide bombers* and the destruction of the World Trade Center are only the start. We must stand firm in battle against fanatic Islam, whether it is from Sunni Fanatics like *Al Qaeda*, or from Shi'ite fanatics like the *Hezbollah!* The *Hezbos*. (Terminology of Rush Limbaugh)

In the 1980s, in the waning years of the Soviet Empire, the Red Army invaded Muslim Afghanistan, installing a communist puppet regime. The only thing that fanatic Islam hates more than the Jews, are atheists. The Soviets sparked a Jihad, and as their empire began to dismember, the Red Army retreated north. They retreated under a hail of shellfire from the Islamic Forces, known as the Mujahedin. A rich Saudi Arabian by the name of Osama Bin Laden, and an Egyptian by the name of Iman Al Zawahiri, a long standing member of the Muslim Brotherhood, led and financed Arab fighters against the Red Army. They founded the network now known as *Al Qaeda*. This is the Arabic word meaning," *The Base.*"

Saddam Hussein, who had been in an eight year long war with the Iranians, ended that bloody war, (which had been marked by the use of chemical weapons) decided to conquer Kuwait. He believed himself to be the reincarnation of King Nebuchadnezzar of Babylon, and sought to rebuild the Babylonian Empire. With the Iraqis massed in Kuwait, and readying for the advance south into Saudi Arabia, Osama Bin Laden offered his fighters from Afghanistan, to drive the Iraqis out. He proposed to do this in the same manner as he had done the Russians in Afghanistan. The King of Saudi Arabia turned instead to the USA, and the U.N. Bin Laden was enraged. To have non-Muslim soldiers on Holy Islamic soil in Arabia was intolerable for Al Qaeda. To him and others like him, the presence of American, British and French soldiers was tantamount to a new crusade against Islam. He declared that the Saudi Royal family must go, and that the United States and Israel, must be destroyed.

Then President, Bill Clinton retreated from the operations in Somalia. Bin Laden and Zawahiri perceived the U.S. to be a paper tiger. It could be destroyed, over a long period of time, by internecine warfare. Jihad was declared and has now spread across the entire globe. Truly we have now entered, the Green Horse of the Apocalypse. Osama bin Laden was killed by U.S. Forces in Pakistan in May of 2011.

How will it all end? Read Isaiah chapter 17, which speaks of a flaming destruction of Damascus Yechezk'el , Ezekiel Chapter 38 and 39. A league of Nations, all of them Islamic, are prophesied to march against the land of Israel.

Yechezk'el 38: 1- 9

> The word of ADONAI came to me: "Human being, turn your face toward Gog (of the land of Magog), chief prince of Meshekh and Tuval; and prophesy against him. Say that Adonai ELOHIM says, 'I am against you, Gog, chief prince of Meshekh and Tuval. I will turn you around, put hooks in your jaws and bring you out with all your army, horses and horsemen, all completely equipped, a great horde with breastplates and shields, all wielding swords. Paras, Ethiopia and Put are with them, all with breastplates and helmets; Gomer with all its troops; the house of Togarmah in the far reaches of the north, with all its troops - many peoples are with you. Prepare yourself, get ready, you and all your crowd gathered around you; and take charge of them. After many days have passed, you will be mustered for service; in later years you will invade the land which has been brought back from the sword, gathered out of many peoples, the mountains of Isra'el. They had been lying in ruins for a long time, but now Isra'el has been extracted from the peoples and all of them are living there securely. You will come up like a storm, you will be like a cloud covering the land - you and all your troops, and many other peoples with you.

Yechezk'el 39 1 – 9

> The word of ADONAI came to me: "Human being, turn your face toward Gog (of the land of Magog), chief prince of Meshekh and Tuval; and prophesy against him. Say that Adonai ELOHIM says, 'I am against you, Gog, chief prince of Meshekh and Tuval. I will turn you around, put hooks in your jaws and bring you out

Yehoiakin ben Ya'ocov

with all your army, horses and horsemen, all completely equipped, a great horde with breastplates and shields, all wielding swords. Paras, Ethiopia and Put are with them, all with breastplates and helmets; Gomer with all its troops; the house of Togarmah in the far reaches of the north, with all its troops - many peoples are with you. Prepare yourself, get ready, you and all your crowd gathered around you; and take charge of them. After many days have passed, you will be mustered for service; in later years you will invade the land which has been brought back from the sword, gathered out of many peoples, the mountains of Isra'el. They had been lying in ruins for a long time, but now Isra'el has been extracted from the peoples and all of them are living there securely. You will come up like a storm, you will be like a cloud covering the land - you and all your troops, and many other peoples with you.

Who are all these nations? These are the Hebrew names of the modern nations of *Iran, Sudan, Libya, Azerbaijan, Turkey,* and the *central Asian states* which have arisen out of the Soviet breakup. All of them are **Muslim**. Verse 13:

Sh'va, D'dan and all the leading merchants of Tarshish will ask you, "Have you come to seize spoil? Have you assembled your hordes to loot; to carry off silver, gold, livestock and other wealth; to take much plunder?'"

Sheba. This is the modern state of Yemen. *Dedan*. This is Saudi Arabia and the Arab states of the Persian Gulf. *Tarshish* is Tunisia. Many of these are part of the OPEC Oil Cartel and all are members of the Arab League. It sounds like they are not part of this terrifying Jihad, led by the Mahdi. The Mahdi is Gog. The Arab states appear to be in great distress over the advance of the Mahdi and are in fear of their economic well being. Verses following speak of a devastating earthquake and speak of how the Mahdi will be destroyed by fire and brimstone. Chaos is within the ranks of the Islamic Army as the Muslims troops turn against each other. Chapter 39 speaks on about it in verses 4 – 6

You will fall on the mountains of Isra'el, you, your troops and all the peoples with you; I will give you to be eaten up by all kinds of birds of prey and by wild animals. You will fall in the open field, for I have spoken,' says Adonai ELOHIM. "'I will also send fire against Magog and against those living securely in the coastlands; then they will know that I am ADONAI.

The remainder of the chapter speaks of what can only be described as a horrific nuclear nightmare, as the Mahdi and his army are incinerated. And it takes seven months to clean up the contamination, which is taken east of the dead sea. Here in a place that will be known as the valley of Hamon Gog, where the trade winds will blow the fallout back over Arabia. And thus will be the final outcome of the 3rd Jihad. We learned in chapter one about the Islamic doctrine that teaches that Yeshua the Messiah (Isa Masih) will return as an ally of the Mahdi and annihilate all who have not so far been converted to Islam under the Mahdi. But all Islam will be shocked when the Messiah returns and destroys both the Mahdi and his false prophet, and all those jihadists who marked themselves with the sign of the Mahdi on their foreheads and left hands. **Behold the Mahdi.**

Appendix II
Is G-d a Trinity?

I want to deal with the subject of my belief concerning the nature of G-d, which came up in the chapter concerning the Christian concept of messiah. Maybe here is where I am going to offend the people who are absolutely dogmatic that G-d is three beings comprising one G-d. The Ancient Holy One is one eternal being and not three. However I may also offend those who are just as dogmatic in the other direction, saying that G-d does not reveal himself in any other way than one single type of manifestation.

"Sh'ma, Yisra'el! ADONAI Eloheinu, ADONAI echad [Hear, Isra'el! ADONAI our God, ADONAI is one] (Devarim (Deuteronomy) 6:4)

Trinitarians will argue and say that the Hebrew word, echad, is a word which means a composite unity. This is not the sense in which the scripture delivers this word. The Ancient Holy One, blessed be His name, is telling us that He is one G-d, and not many like the pagans of the world had been deceived into believing by Satan'el (the Devil) and his evil host. Judgment had just been made against the Principalities in the Spirit realm which had dominated Egypt such as Ammun Ra. This is an emphatic declaration of the unity of G-d, and there is no way around it The sense of the word, *"echad"* here is alone, one and one only.

Here is a good quotation on this verse from the Stone Chumash, page 973, which is good illustration of this concept.

> **Echad** – One. We perceive G-d in many ways – He is kind, angry, merciful, wise, judgmental – and these apparently contradictory manifestations convinced some ancient and medieval philosophers that there must be many gods. But the Torah says that Hashem

is the *"One and Only"* – there is an inner harmony for all that He does, though human intelligence cannot comprehend what it is. This will be understood and the End of Days, when G-d's ways are illuminated. Rabbi Gedaliah Schorr likened this concept to a ray of light seen through a prism. Though the viewer sees a myriad of different colors, it is a single ray of light. So to, G-d's many manifestations are truly one. (Stone Chumash, Artscroll-Mesorah Heritage Foundation)

The next thing they say is that the word *"Elohim"* implies the Trinity. This is not the case. This is the most frequent Hebrew word for G-d, and is used over 2,500 times in the Tanakh. The root of this word is *"El"* or *"Eloah."* The word *"Elohim"* is plural in form and this is the argument that is used to support the Trinity theory. However it is singular in construction (used with a singular verb or adjective). This term is often applied to heathen gods (Shemot 18:11; 20:3; B'reshite 35:2; Yehoshua 24:20) and also of Angels (Tehillim 8:5; 97:7; Iyov 1:6) When used in these senses, it is plural in form, but never when applying to G-d. Yeshua, our Rabbi King Messiah used a form of this when he was nailed up on a Roman execution stake.

At about three, Yeshua uttered a loud cry, "Eli! Eli! L'mah sh'vaktani? (My God! My God! Why have you deserted me?)["Matisyahu 27:45]

Remember that the scripture, when read in any translation other than the original Hebrew, cannot grasp the complexity and the subtle nuances of the Holy Tongue itself.

In some Christian circles there are those who use the spiritual tradition of Judaism, known as Kabbalah to support the doctrine of the Trinity supposing that it comes from ancient forms of Judaism. But the works of Kabbalah such as the **Bahir, Zohar** and **Sefer Yetserah** do not support the trinity, but rather the concept stated by Rabbi Gedaliah Schorr in his analogy of light viewed through a prism. When you see one single beam of light through a prism, you can see how the ray is multifaceted. The same holds true with the Mystical writings of the *Merkavah* (Heavenly Chariot) and those of the Essenes.

If G-d is a Trinity, then where does this verse play into that?

Out of the throne proceed lightnings, sounds, and thunders. There were seven lamps of fire burning before the throne, which are the seven Spirits of God. (Hisgalus [Revelation] 4:5)

This is explained in the Tanakh by the Prophet Yeshayahu.

There shall come forth a netzer out of the stock of Yishai, and a branch out of his roots shall bear fruit. The *Spirit of the LORD* shall rest on him, the *spirit of wisdom* and *understanding*, the *spirit of counsel* and *might*, the *spirit of knowledge* and of the *fear of the LORD* (Yeshayahu [Isaiah] 11:1 – 2)

It is obvious that all of these are part of the knowable aspects of the Ancient Holy One, blessed be His Name, and are not seven different beings making up one G-d. The same is true of what Yeshua said when he spoke of Immersion as part of the conversion of Gentiles to Messianic Judaism.

Yeshua came to them and spoke to them, saying, "All authority has been given to me in heaven and on eretz. Go, and make talmidim of all nations, immersing them in *the name of the Father and of the Son and of the Ruach HaKodesh*, teaching them to observe all things which I commanded you. Behold, I am with you always, even to the end of the age." Amein (Matisyahu 28: 18 – 20)

Here he is speaking of the Sacred name of the One G-d, **YHVH**. Not three separate entities. Rabbi King Messiah frequently speaks of the deep mysteries of the Ancient of Days. He expresses them in simple human terms that we are more likely to understand. I am in no way trying to limit G-d.. Is Yeshua the son of G-d? Yes He is. Is he Messiah? Yes He is!. Is he a mere man or a super prophet appointed by G-d? No He is not a mere man and yes He is a super prophet appointed by G-d.! He is part of the living G-d incarnated as flesh, which explains why in this knowable aspect, He can call himself the *"Son of G-d."* Does that mean that G-d is three entities, no it does not. There is language in the Bible which shows that the one G-d revealed himself in the way that trinitarians express it, and then there is the fact established in the Torah that G-d is one being.

I believe that mainstream Judaism is also trying to limit G_d, when they declare that He never manifested himself in a human form. They too have an agenda just as the trinitarians do. For the Orthodox and the other non-Messianic forms of Judaism to declare that Messianics are not Jews because we believe that Rabbi King Messiah is/was Yeshua ha Notzri (Jesus of Nazareth) and that the Ancient Holy One could not put a part of himself into a human form is just another form of dogma that puts G-d into a box!

The doctrine of the trinity is a simplified view of a complex, unknowable G-d. *(Ein Sof)* Even the unitarian view, which is my own, cannot grasp the Almighty Creator. No one can know G-d, which is why Rabbi King Messiah said this to Rabbi Nakdimon;

If I told you earthly things and you don't believe, how will you believe if I tell you heavenly things? No one has ascended into heaven, but he who descended out of heaven, the Son of Man, who is in heaven. (Yochanan 3: 12 – 13)

Here is another wonder of the Ancient Holy One, blessed be His Name. The first Messianics were celebrating Shavuot fifty days after Rabbi King Messiah's last Pesach Seder when Hashem touched all of them at once. This scripture is very important and we will be referring to it again in this study.

> Now when the day of Shavu'ot had come, they were all with one accord in one place. Suddenly there came from the sky a sound like the rushing of a mighty wind, and it filled all the house where they were sitting. Tongues like fire appeared and were distributed to them, and it sat on each one of them. (Acts 2: 1 – 3)

How can One G-d rest on multiple people? He can because The Ancient Holy One, blessed be His Name, is omnipresent, and his unique oneness is beyond our comprehension. A good earthly analogy would be this. The Oceans of the earth are all one body of water. Yet it is revealed in several parts under different names (Aspects) known as; Pacific, Atlantic, Mediterranean, Indian and Arctic. Under this one great body of water lay many mountains, all covered by one body of water. Thus G-d as a singularity, can manifest his nature as *Father* (Ein Sof or Keter [Crown]) *Son, Holy Spirit, Hokmah*, (wisdom) *Binah* (understanding) *Da'at* (Knowledge) *Hesed* (Grace and love) *Gevurah* (Power and judgment or *Din*), *Tiferet* (Beauty, *Yesod* (Foundation) and *Malkut* (physical Kingdom or manifestation). These are_many manifestations of one eternal G-d, and he can cover all of creation, let alone the Talmidim (Disciples) of Rabbi King Messiah at Shavuot. There is no simplification of the nature of the Spirit of the Ancient of Days, our beloved G-d.

Appendix III
SALVATION

In this appendix we will be discussing the issue of salvation. I felt that was very important to discuss this topic in a book which deals with t concepts of messiah, to illustrate the Messianic Jewish concept of salvation. This word has a specific meaning in evangelical Christian doctrines which is, trust in the Lord Jesus and have eternal life, going to heaven when you die. But there is more to it than that. Is being a son of G-d the same as salvation? Is, believing, the only step to salvation? What does it mean to be "saved'? We will explore these topics in this section.

Defining the requirements

The Bible gives a clear definition of the requirements for salvation. What is clear, is that it is through faith and has always been so. Many people believe that the Sages of Judaism taught that salvation was through works and the keeping of Torah mitzvot (instructions) but this is not the case. They have always taught that the Ancient of Days required a person have faith. It is even written concerning Avraham Avinu believed G-d and because of this he was declared to be righteous.

Then what should we say Avraham, our forefather, obtained by his own efforts? For if Avraham came to be considered righteous by God because of legalistic observances, then he has something to boast about. But this is not how it is before God! For what does the Tanakh say? "Avraham put his trust in God, and it was credited to his account as righteousness. [Roman ch 4: 1 - 3]

In the book of Acts we have the following statement which takes into consideration not just the head of the home but his family as well. The messiah is declared to be the means of salvation.

"Therefore, brothers, let it be known to you that through this man is proclaimed forgiveness of sins! That is, God clears everyone who puts his trust in this man, even in regard to all the things concerning which you could not be cleared by the Torah of Moshe.[Acts 13: 38 -39]

Later we find Rav Sha'ul and Sila have been cast into prison:

Around midnight, Sha'ul and Sila were praying and singing hymns to God, while the other prisoners listened attentively. Suddenly there was a violent earthquake which shook the prison to its foundations. All the doors flew open and everyone's chains came loose. The jailer awoke, and when he saw the doors open he drew his sword and was about to kill himself, for he assumed that the prisoners had escaped. But Sha'ul shouted, "Don't harm yourself! We're all here!" Calling for lights, the jailer ran in, began to tremble and fell down in front of Sha'ul and Sila. Then, leading them outside, he said, "Men, what must I do to be saved?" They said, "Trust in the Lord Yeshua, and you will be saved - you and your household!" Whereupon they told him and everyone in his household the message about the Lord. Then, even at that late hour of the night, the jailer took them and washed off their wounds; and without delay, he and all his people were immersed. After that, he brought them up to his house and set food in front of them; and he and his entire household celebrated their having come to trust in God [Acts chapter 16:25 – 34]

What did Yeshua the Messiah himself say?

16 "For God so loved the world that he gave his only and unique Son, so that everyone who trusts in him may have eternal life, instead of being utterly destroyed.[Yochanan 3:16.]

Time for definitions. The Hebrew word for salvation is *"Yeshuah"* and the Greek word is *"Soterion"*. This word in the Bible is not always a a technical theological term, but simply denotes deliverance from almost any kind of evil, whether material or spiritual. Theologically however it denotes the process by which the Ancient Holy One, blessed be His

Name, delivers mankind from all that interferes with the enjoyment of the highest blessings which He bestows.

Bible passages

The following list comes from Wikipedia. I have adapted it myself by changing the names Jesus, to Yeshua, and his title from, Christ, to Messiah.

The New International Version of the New Testament contains 138 verses that with the words "salvation" (45), "save" (41) or "saved" (52). The following are some of the New Testament passages most cited in this regard:

- *Belief and baptism*:
    - "Whoever believes and is baptized will be saved, but whoever does not believe will be condemned."[Mk. 16:16]
    - "…all of us who were baptized into Messiah Yeshua were baptized into his death. We were therefore buried with him through baptism into death so that, just as Messiah was raised from the dead through the glory of the Father, we too may live a new life."[Rom. 6:3-5]
    - "Peter replied, "Repent and be baptized, every one of you, in the name of Messiah Yeshua for the forgiveness of your sins. And you will receive the gift of the Holy Spirit."[Acts. 2:38]
    - "Yeshua replied, "Let it be so now; it is proper for us to do this to fulfill all righteousness." Then Yochanan consented."[Mt. 3:15]
    - "In reply Jesus declared, "I tell you the truth, no one can see the kingdom of God unless he is born again."[Jn. 3:3]

- "After this, Yeshua and his disciples went out into the Judean countryside, where he spent some time with them, and baptized."[Jn. 3:22]

- "For you have been born again, not of perishable seed, but of imperishable, through the living and enduring word of God".

- *Belief in Yeshua*:

  - "For God so loved the world that he gave his one and only Son, that whoever believes in him shall not perish but have eternal life."[Jn. 3:16]

  - "Salvation is found in no one else, for there is no other name given under heaven by which we must be saved."[Ac. 4:12]

- *Born again:* "Yeshua replied, 'Very truly I tell you, no one can see the kingdom of God without being born again... Very truly I tell you, no one can enter the kingdom of God without being born of water and the Spirit.'"[Jn. 3:3-5]

- *"If you declare with your mouth, 'Yeshua is Lord,' and believe in your heart that God Confession and belief:*

  - raised him from the dead, you will be saved. For it is with your heart that you believe and are justified, and it is with your mouth that you profess your faith and are saved."[Rom. 10:9-10]

  - "For whosoever shall call upon the name of the Lord shall be saved."[Rom. 10:13]

- *Gift of God through Messiah:*

  - *"For the wages of sin is death; but the gift of God is eternal life through Yeshua Messiah our Lord."[Rom. 6:23]*

- "...And to this day it is said, "On the mountain of the LORD it will be provided."[Gen. 22:14] Calvary

- *Forgiving others necessary:* "If you forgive others when they sin against you, your heavenly Father will also forgive you. But if you do not forgive others their sins, your Father will not forgive your sins.[Matt. 6:14-15]

- *God's love*:

  - "God demonstrates His own love for us in this: While we were still sinners, Messiah died for us."[Rom. 5:8]

  - "But because of his great love for us, God, who is rich in mercy, made us alive with Messiah even when we were dead in transgressions—it is by grace you have been saved."[Eph. 2:4-5]

  - "When the kindness and love of God our Savior appeared, he saved us, not because of righteous things we had done, but because of his mercy. He saved us through the washing of rebirth and renewal by the Holy Spirit, whom he poured out on us generously through Yeshua Messiah our Savior...."[Titus]3:4-6

- *Judged by works:* "And I saw the dead, great and small, standing before the throne, and books were opened. Another book was opened, which is the book of life. The dead were judged according to what they had done as recorded in the books. The sea gave up the dead that were in it, and death and Hades gave up the dead that were in them, and everyone was judged according to what they had done."[Rev. 20:12-13]

- *Repentance and baptism:* "Peter replied, 'Repent and be baptized, every one of you, in the name of Jesus Christ for the forgiveness of your sins. And you will receive the gift of the Holy Spirit.'"[Acts 2:38]

- *Salvation and works:* "You see that people are justified by what they do and not by faith alone."[Jas. 2:24] This verse and the surrounding passage is disputed, centering primarily on the meaning of the word *justified*.

- *Salvation by God's Grace, not by works:*

- "For it is by grace you have been saved, through faith—and this is not from yourselves, it is the gift of God—not by works, so that no one can boast."[Eph. 2:8-9]

- "He saved us, not because of righteous things we had done, but because of his mercy. He saved us through the washing of rebirth and renewal by the Holy Spirit whom he poured out on us generously through Yeshua Messiah our Savior, so that, having been justified by his grace, we might become heirs having the hope of eternal life."[Titus 3:5-7]

- "When the kindness of God our Saviour, and his love towards us, appeared, not by works done in righteousness, which we did ourselves, but according to his mercy he *saved* us, through the washing of regeneration and renewing of the Holy Spirit, which he poured out upon us richly, through Yeshua Messiah our Saviour; that, being justified by his grace, we might be made heirs according to the hope of eternal life."[Titus 3:4-7]

- *Salvation as an ongoing process:* "To us who *are being saved*, (the word of the cross) is the power of God."[1 Cor 1:18]

- *Salvation as yet to be obtained:* "Since, therefore, we are now justified by (Messiah's) blood, much more *shall we be saved* by him from the wrath of God."[Rom. 5:9]

- *Salvation as a narrow path:* "Wide is the gate, and broad the way, that leads to destruction, and many go in there:

because strait is the gate and narrow is the way that leads to life, and few there be that find it....[Mt. 7:13-14]

- *Sin separates humanity from God.*
- "For all have sinned and fall short of the glory of God."[Rom. 3:23]
- "Therefore, just as sin entered the world through one man, and death through sin, and in this way death came to all people, because all sinned...." [Rom. 5:12]

Trust and Intent

Complete trust in G-d is the most important of human conditions for salvation. The Ancient of Days, blessed be His Name, wants us to observe his Torah However the Ancient Holy One, blessed be His Name, is not satisfied with a mere legalistic observations. After salvation he wants us to observe it with *"Kavenah"* or, *"Intent of heart."* Kavenah is going to be a natural prerequisite for salvation for if a person has no intent of heart to begin with, then the Ancient Holy One, blessed be His Name, will not force that person to accept His free gift.

But is believing the only step? What does it say in the book of Romans chapter 10?

Brothers, my heart's deepest desire and my prayer to God for Isra'el is for their salvation; for I can testify to their zeal for God. But it is not based on correct understanding; for, since they are unaware of God's way of making people righteous and instead seek to set up their own, they have not submitted themselves to God's way of making people righteous. For the goal at which the Torah aims is the Messiah, who offers righteousness to everyone who trusts. For Moshe writes about the righteousness grounded in the Torah that the person who does these things will attain life through them. Moreover, the righteousness grounded in trusting says: "Do not say in your heart, 'Who will ascend to heaven?'" that is, to bring the Messiah down - or, "'Who will descend into she'ol?'" that is, to bring the Messiah up from the dead. What, then, does it say? "The word is near you, in your mouth and in your heart."1 that is, the word about trust which we proclaim, namely, that if you acknowledge publicly with your mouth that Yeshua is Lord and trust in your heart that God raised him from the dead, you will be delivered. For with the heart one goes on trusting and thus continues toward righteousness, while with the mouth one keeps on making public acknowledgment and thus continues toward deliverance. For the pas sage quoted says that everyone who rests his trust on him will not be humiliated. That means that there is no difference between Jew and Gentile - ADONAI is the same for everyone, rich toward everyone who calls on him, since everyone who calls on the name of ADONAI will be delivered. But how can they call on someone if they haven't trusted in him? And how can they trust in someone if they haven't heard about him? And how can they hear about someone if no one is proclaiming him? And how can people proclaim him unless God sends them? - as the Tanakh puts it, "How beautiful are the feet of those announcing good news about good things!" The problem is that they haven't all paid attention to the Good News and obeyed it. For Yesha'yahu says, "ADONAI, who has trusted what he has heard from us?" So trust comes from what is heard, and what is heard comes through a word proclaimed about the Messiah. "But, I say, isn't it rather that they didn't hear?" No, they did hear "Their voice has gone out throughout the whole world and their words to the ends of the earth." "But, I say, isn't it rather that Isra'el didn't understand?" "I will provoke you to jealousy over a non-nation, over a nation void of understanding I will make you angry." Moreover, Yesha'yahu boldly says, "I was found by those who were not looking for me, I became known to those who did not ask for me"; but to Isra'el he says, "All day long I held out my hands to a people who kept disobeying and contradicting."

Concepts of Messiah

One can believe something is, but not necessarily have trust. Satan'el knows and believes that Yeshua is the Messiah but that belief in and of itself does not mean that Satan'el is saved. Look at the verses quoted above and analyze them. What are we to do? The WORD. This is not meaning that we are observant for legalistic purposes, thinking that by mere observances of the Torah without *Kavenah,* are bringing salvation. No. The verses explain that we must trust and acknowledge publicly because what is truly in your heart is then spoken publicly by mouth. Only on this basis can doing the word lead to being made righteous and thereby our deliverance from the penalty of death. According to Dr David Stern in his Jewish New Testament Commentary on page 400;

> In fact, verse 9 plus the last two verses cited constitute the who Gospel in brief, so far as the individual is concerned. As a sinner you not only fall short of earning G-d's praise (3:23) but have earned death as your wages (6:23a). Nevertheless, G-d's free gift to you is eternal life through Yeshua the Messiah, our Lord (6:23b). If you put your trust in him inwardly (heart) and outwardly (mouth), you will be delivered from death to life (verse 9).

The Greek word for **"to acknowledge publicly"** is *"omologein"* usually translated, "to confess" but meaning literally, "to say the same thing" in this case, to agree with what G-d has revealed in his word about himself and His son.(JNTC, JNTP Dr David Stern)

Verse 9 speaks about an event in ones life at a definite time or moment and the implication given in verse 10 is that we must always continue in trust and acknowledging our faith in public. Being not in a state of denial. But by far the most important is that our faith in Yeshua must come with the conviction in our hearts that he has been raised from the dead. For if he is not, then he cannot fulfill the prophecies which yet remain for him.

So our trust in Yeshua is much more than the intellectual acknowledgment that he walked the earth. It is complete reliance upon Rabbi King Messiah as the word of life putting your trust in his name. When you trust in someones name, this means that you are trusting in everything that a person is. So if you believe as I do that Rabbi King Messiah is a knowable aspect of Hashem, then you are putting your trust in all that the name of G-d implies

Does this make one a child of G-d.? Shliach Yochanan's(Apostle John's) book says in chapter 1:12

But to as many as did receive him, to those who put their trust in his person and power, he gave the right to become children of God, not because of bloodline, physical impulse or human intention, but because of God.

In a sense all people are children of G-d because it was He who created us. The Ancient Holy One, blessed be His name, speaks of himself in numerous places throughout the scripture is a father and in Yeshayahu 49:14- 15 as a mother. But the sense we get out of the verses above are that being a child of G-d means that a person is has an intimate personal relationship with the Ancient of Days like the Patriarchs did as well as Moshe and King David. So to simply just being saved does not make you a spiritual child of G-d. Yes you are covered by his saving grace but without getting to know him, a person has not exercised the **"right"** which he has been given to be a child of G-d, in the sense that the verse above indicates.

Defining the meaning.

What does it mean to be saved? What are we being saved from? Certainly not from all the pain and heartaches that come to us in the *Olam Hazeh* (present world). A quick glance at the history of persecutions and pogroms against true believers and followers of Rabbi King Messiah will attest to this. Being saved is the restoration of eternal life that was lost at the fall in Gan Eden. A person may be saved and yet not be a son of G-d, as I have stated earlier. Not living a life in Torah shows that a person is not a child of G-d, even though they might be indeed saved. Just getting the power to become a son, does not mean that one will become a son of G-d. To do so he must live the life that the Ancient Holy One, blessed be His Name, has prescribed in the Bible, showing that he is a workman, and that he is showing his faith by his actions.

What are we being saved from? We are being saved from separation from the Ancient Holy One and his judgment of evil at the end of days. What is evil? It is the dark and heinous crimes of both mankind and the fallen Angels, which come from an absolute deep and willful disdain of all that is righteous and given to us for life by the Ancient Holy One, blessed be His Name. Eternal death is separation from the Ancient of Days, while eternal life is union and abiding with those knowable aspects of Hashem, which we can see without being taken from existence. The *Ein Sof* is that aspect we call, "Father" and Yeshua in a great mystical statement dealing with the nature of G-d said; "No one has seen the Father except He who came from the Father."

The Greek word which is used most often in the Brit Hadashah for being saved can be found in Strong's Exhaustive Concordance of the Bible. "**Soteria**" (Strong's number 4991) and means; rescue or safety or to be delivered. Salvation. Also "**Soterion**" (Strong's number 4992) which can mean, defender or defense, and salvation.

Salvation is also Corporate.

In our western American culture, the individual is prized. We hear a lot about the value of the individual person, and not so much the community. Thus the doctrine of salvation of the individual person has been emphasized above that of the community or people as a whole. Take a look at the story of the Roman Jailer. What did Rav Sha'ul say to him?

The jailer awoke, and when he saw the doors open he drew his sword and was about to kill himself, for he assumed that the prisoners had escaped. But Sha'ul shouted, "Don't harm yourself! We're all here!" Calling for lights, the jailer ran in, began to tremble and fell down in front of Sha'ul and Sila. Then, leading them outside, he said, "Men, what must I do to be saved?" They said, "Trust in the Lord Yeshua, and you will be saved - you and your household!" Whereupon they told him and everyone in his household the message about the Lord. Then, even at that late hour of the night, the jailer took them and washed off their wounds; and without delay, he and all his people were immersed. After that, he brought them up to his house and set food in front of them; and he and his entire household celebrated their having come to trust in God. [Acts 13:17 – 35]

Look and see that when the Jailer received salvation, his family chose to join him and they benefited from the fact that the father had chosen to be saved. He was spiritual reborn in the manner which Yeshua King Messiah spoke of to Rabbi Nakdimon (Nicodemus). The minor children fell under the cover of their reborn father, because they also chose to follow Messiah. The whole household was now benefiting from salvation. This is true today as well. But however when others in the household reject the call and see no need of being saved, they then of course do not benefit from the Father and Mother's salvation, because they now rebel against the parents in this regard.

It is a fact that the Jewish people emphasize community over single individuals. Many people who proclaim Messiah to the non-Messianic Jews often offer a Gospel which is so oriented to the individual, that it ignores the corporate, and is thus inadequate. The Jewish people have a strong sense of nationality and to them, a purely individualistic approach to salvation, ignoring the corporate body of the Jewish people seems to them selfish. A study of the Hebrew word, **"Yeshuah"** (Salvation) and how it is used in the Hebrew Scriptures will show you that salvation is never thought of as being just simply for individuals, but for Israel as a nation.

Summary.

What I find very special in this whole concept of salvation, is the fact that the Ancient of Days, blessed be His Name, does not wish anyone to perish at the End of Days. It is wonderful to me to think of the Ancient of Days Himself wants to restore to us tat eternal life that was lost at the fall. So limitless is He, that YHVH flowed down his emanations of life-force of Tiferet (Beauty). This beauty became Malchut (physical kingdom, king, or realm) which became a body men could see and call, Rabbi King Messiah. He then gave it in sacrifice so that that eternal life would be restored. Give Him a chance, and accept him as Messiah and be filled with his love.

Bibliography

Islamic Source material

Understanding the Hadith;The Sacred Traditions of Islam, Ram Swarup,Prometheus Books, 2002

Islam. A Short History. Karen Armstrong, The Modern Library, 2002

Sahih Muslim. English translation by Abdul Hamid Siddiqi in four volumes. Lahore: Sh Muhammad Ashraf, 1975.

Tirmizi Sharif Urdu translation in two volumes by Lal Kuan. Delhi: Rabbani Book Depot, 1980.

Sahih Bukhari Sharif. Churiwalan, Delhi: Kitab Khana, Ishait'l Islam.

Mishkatu'-l Masbih (Niche of Lamps) Seven-hundred-year-old collection of Hadis, very popular and much in use. Reprint of English translation by Dr. James Robson. Lahore:Sh. Muhammad Ashraf, 1973. Urdu translation in 2 volumes;Delhi; Rabbani Book Depot.

The Conept of the Mahdi in Sunni Islam..Arjomand, Said Amir (Dec. 2007)

Muhammad ibn Ibrahim Nomani: (Sheikh Muhammad ibn Ibrahim Nomani, al-Ghaybah al-Nomani,p.

Muhammad ibn Ibrahim Nomani:

Sheikh Muhammad bin Ibrahim Nomani, al-Ghaybah al-Nomani, p.189

Bihar al-Anwar: **51**: 146

Muhammad ibn Ibrahim Nomani: 189 (Sheikh Muhammad ibn Ibrahim Nomani, al-Ghaybah al-Nomani,p. 189

Muhammad ibn Ibrahim Nomani: 191

Ja'far al-Sadiq

Mugahi, Abdul-Rahim.The Awaited Savier of Humanity (Al Mahdi in the Eyes of the Ahul Bayt. The Islamic Education Board of the World Federation of Khoja Shia Ithna-Asheri Muslim Communities. http://www.al-islam.org/40ahadith-twelfthimam/.

For the Qur'an, there are the following good translations,

GLORIOUS QU'RAN. English translation with the original Arabic text by Abdullah Yusuf Al Daral-Kitab al Masri.

QU'RAN MAJEED. Hindi and English translations with original text in Arabic; English translation by M. Pickthall. Rampur: Maktab Al-Hasnat.

THE KORAN. Translated by E. H. Palmer. London, New York, and Toronto: Oxford University Press.

Jewish Source Material

The Mishna, Talmud, Midrash, and the Zohar. They are quite voluminous and so if one wants to enrich their lives by studying the Rabbinic literature, I recommend the following excellent works;

- Every Man's Talmud. Abraham Cohen Schocken Books, New York 1995. Original Publication in 1949

- The Talmud. H. Polano. 1876, Claxton Remsen & Haffelfinger. Philadelphia. Reprint 2003, The Book Tree.

- The Cambridge Companion to the Talmud and Rabbinic Literature. Edited by Charlotte

- Elisheva Fonrobert and Martin S. Jaffee. Cambridge University Press. 2007

- Teach Yourself Judaism. C.M. Pilkington and Jonathan Gorsky. 1995, 2000, 2003

- The Essential Zohar. Rav P.S. Berg. Bell Tower, New York, 2002

- The Mishnah. An Introduction. Jacob Neusner 1989. Jason Aronson Inc. Northvale, N.J. & London

- The Midrash. An Introduction. Jacob Nuesner. 1990. Jason Aronson Inc. Northvale, N.J. & London

- The Mishnah. Religious Perspectives. Jacob Nuesner. Brill Academic Publishers, Inc. Boston. Lieden

- 2002.

- Jesus In the Talmud. Peter Schafer Princeton University Press Princeton and Oxford 2007

- The Stone Edition, The Chumash, 1998 by Mesorah Publications, Ltd

- Jewish Jewels, Yom Kippur Issue 2010

- Korem. Herz Homburg, 1818

If you wish to aquire translations of the Rabbinic Literature and study it, Artscroll publishes very fine books, which are affordable, yet works of art. That is with the exception of the *Zohar*. Soncino Press produced a fine translation, which was translated by *Paul Fievel Levertoff,* who was a graduate of the prestigious Volozhin Yeshiva in Lithuania. He was an Orthodox Jew with Chasidic ancestry from Orsha, Belarus. He was one of the first *Messianic Rabbis* of the modern age. Another outstanding translation of the Zohar is by Daniel Matt. The Pritzker addition of the Zohar by Daniel Matt is an ongoing project. As of this writing, seven volumes are available. Be warned though, all of these works are greater than the size of Encyclopedia Britannica and it is quite an expensive undertaking.

Christian source material

- Come Out of Her My People. C.J. Koster

- Catechism of the Catholic Church – English translation (U.S.A., 2nd edition) (English translation of the *Catechism of the Catholic Church: Modifications from the Editio Typica*, copyright 1997, United States Catholic Conference, Inc., Libreria Editrice Vaticana) (Glossary and *Index Analyticus*, copyright 2000, U.S. Catholic Conference, Inc.). ISBN-1-57455-110-8

- *Compendium of the Catechism of the Catholic Church* – English translation (USCCB, 2006). ISBN 1-57455-720-3

- United States Catholic Catechism for Adults – English "... resource for preparation of catechumens in the Rite of Christian Initiation of Adults and for ongoing catechesis of adults" (USCCB, 2006). ISBN 1-57455-450-6

- Holden, A. (2002) (PDF). *Cavorting With the Devil. Jehovah's Witnesses who abandon their faith.* Department of Sociology, Lancaster University, Lancaster LA1 4YL, UK. p. Endnote [i]. http://www.lancs.ac.uk/fass/sociology/papers/holden-cavorting-with-the-devil.pdf. Retrieved 2009-06-21.

- Alan Rogerson (1969). *Millions Now Living Will Never Die.* Constable. p. 87.

- Beckford, James A. (1975). *The Trumpet of Prophecy: A Sociological Study of Jehovah's Witnesses.* Oxford: Basil Blackwell. pp. 105. ISBN-0-631-16310-7.

- *Revelation Its Grand Climax*, Watch Tower Bible & Tract Society, 1988, pg 36, "In the songbook produced by Jehovah's people in 1905, there were twice as many songs praising Jesus as there were songs praising Jehovah God. In their 1928 songbook, the number of songs extolling Jesus was about the same as the number extolling Jehovah. But in the latest songbook of 1984, Jehovah is honored by four times as many songs as is Jesus. This is in harmony with Jesus' own words: 'The Father is greater than I am.' Love for Jehovah must be preeminent, accompanied by deep love for Jesus and appreciation of his precious sacrifice and office as God's High Priest and King."

- Alan Rogerson (1969). *Millions Now Living Will Never Die.* Constable. p. 90.

- Hoekema, Anothona A. (1963). *The Four Major Cults.* Grand Rapids, Michigan: William B. Eerdmans. pp. 262. ISBN -0-8028-3117-6.

- Penton, M.J. (1997). *Apocalypse Delayed.* University of Toronto Press. p. 372. ISBN -0-8020-7973-3,978082079732

- "Stay in the "City of Refuge" and Live!", *The Watchtower*, November 15, 1995, page 19

- Insight on the Scriptures Volume 2 p. 362 Mediator "Those for Whom Christ Is Mediator"

- http://mormonnewsroom.org

Historical and other Source Material

Much of the historical narrative ion this book come from my own very extensive reading of history over many years. There are no direct quotes from any book of history, but there are allusions and mentions made to various historical works. I have listed these as well as other books and sources from where the reader my obtain additional facts about the historical narratives presented in this book.

- The Works of Josephus. Translated by William Whiston, Hendickson Publishers, 1987

- The Book of Jubilees. Translated by R.H. Charles. The Book Tree, 2003

- The Forgotten Books of Eden, Alpha House, 1927

- The Illustrated Atlas of Jewish Civilization, Quantum Books, 2005

- Atlas of World History,Philips,1999

- End Times with Walid Shoebat video series, www.shoebat.com

- Messianic Judaism 101. Audio Teachings by Messianic Jewish Pastor John Popp, Beth Shalom Messianic Fellowship,P.O. Box 3170, Coeur d' Alene, Idaho, 83816. Produced by Bet Doresh Messianic Jewish Ministries of New Mexico. jehoiakin@yahoo.com

- Constantine The Great. The Man and His Times,Michael Grant, Macmillan, 1994

Printed in Great Britain
by Amazon